Free on The Inside

The Life of a Missionary POW

Free on the Inside

The Life of a Missionary POW

Written by
Chung Yeun-Hee

Translated by
Hoyeon Choi and Gordon Timbers

Colorado Springs • Milton Keynes • Hyderabad

The proceeds from this book will go to the Yanbian University of Science and Technology, Jilin, China.

Authentic Publishing
A Ministry of Biblica
We welcome your questions and comments.

USA	1820 Jet Stream Drive, Colorado Springs, CO 80921 www.authenticbooks.com
UK	9 Holdom Avenue, Bletchley, Milton Keynes, Bucks, MK1 1QR www.authenticmedia.co.uk
India	Logos Bhavan, Medchal Road, Jeedimetla Village, Secunderabad 500 055, A.P.

Free on the Inside
ISBN-13: 978-1-60657-013-5

11 10 09 / 6 5 4 3 2 1

Published in 2009 by Authentic

A catalog record for this book is available through the Library of Congress.

Cover design: Dan Jamison
Interior design: projectluz.com
Editorial team: Kay Larson, Daniel Johnson, John Dunham

Printed in the United States of America

Contents

EDITOR'S NOTE

Free on the Inside, known as *My Cup Overflows* in Korea, has been a classic for the generations that have read it since it was first published in 1981. The main character, Mang Eui-Soon, is virtually a household name. He was the consummate patriot at the outbreak of the Korean War, wondering why brothers were killing each other and seeking to reconcile people. He was also a devout Christian who charged people to live peaceably serving one another as servants of Jesus.

To Koreans, Mang Eui-Soon is much like Jim Elliott is to American Christians. It may take a moment of prompting ("You know, the guys who flew into the jungle in South America and were killed by the tribe . . ."), but most will say, "Oh, he was such an amazing man!" After *My Cup Overflows*, inspired by Mang Eui-Soon's life, was penned by a popular novelist and later staged as a critically acclaimed opera, his life became a fixture in the Korean imagination.

In Korea, *My Cup Overflows* is known as a novel that is based on a true story. No one doubts that it is a true story. However in America, there is more suspicion about the word "novel" and the value it has for conveying a biographical account. The author, Chung Yeun-Hee, researched her book extensively, interviewing family, friends, and acquaintances and consulting letters to accurately represent Mang Eui-Soon's story. Thirty years after the events, she approached her task with the rigor of a biographer. She created a limited number of characters and events to flesh out the story. She also changed some names to protect people who would not want to be identified in the story for various reasons. The translators have added relevant Korean history to help Western readers place the story in context.

As the publisher of the abridged English edition, we wrestled with whether to call this book a biography, fiction, historical fiction, or a novel. In the end, we feel that this book is more biography than novel, as the author has represented Mang Eui-Soon's character and story truly and accurately, even in situations that she created to show how he would have interacted with those around him.

Mang Eui-Soon's story is powerful and life-changing. We hope you enjoy it as much as we did.

John Dunham
Managing Editor
Authentic

TRANSLATOR'S NOTE

One Sunday afternoon I was looking for reading materials at leisure in our small church library. I was attracted to a paperback entitled *My Cup Overflows* in Korean. I started to read it there and then took it home. When I finished, day was dawning, and I found my eyes running with tears. I was held spellbound by this young man who served those prisoners of war whose bodies and spirits were brutalized by war. I dared to start to translate without calculating my capability in English. I have never had professional writing training, and the task was enormous. As the translation progressed, I had an opportunity to discuss the project with Reverend Gordon Timbers, who was then a guest speaker at our English Speaking Ministry, London Korean Christian Church, London, Ontario, Canada. He showed genuine interest, and we worked together. It took over ten years to complete. I felt like an archaeologist excavating artifacts buried deep underground. In telling this story, the author, Chung Yeun-Hee, gives a poignant and evocative portrayal of the human spirit overcoming the devastating effects of war. I also appreciated the author's lyrical description of the main character and the physical environment. This Korean edition has been on all-time Christian bestseller lists in Korea during the last two decades. Fifty-nine years after the

Korean War, North Korea now draws international attention because of development of a nuclear bomb. This story takes us into a forgotten corner of modern history.

My thanks go to the author, Ms. Chung Yeun-Hee, for allowing me to translate one of her most reputable novels and to Reverend Gordon Timbers for sharing in this project to help bring it to completion.

As I complete my work on this project, I thank many people who contributed to the translation of this book: my wife, Su-Ok Choi, my family members Sandra, my son-in-law Dr. Juno Park, Abraham, daughter-in-law Dorothy Choi (Kim), and my brother-in-law Professor Nam Song-Woo, Pukyong National University, Busan, Korea, for their prayers, advice, and encouragement; Mrs. Elsie Lunn for her willingness to discuss this story with me throughout this work and to carefully read and correct a draft of the novel; Dr. Regina Joyce Clark for her passion for this book, encouragement, and excellent editing; my heartfelt thanks go out to Rev. Dr. Park Jae-Hoon who has encouraged, excited, and genuinely discussed this work and provided a team photo of the Wilderness Church members and sermon notes from Mang Eui-Soon; Professor Young Yoo, University of Toronto, for his insights about Korean history and updating me on the geography of Korea; Professor R. W. L. Guisso, University of Toronto, for his comments and encouragement; Mr. Ray Wiseman for sharing his expertise on publication and for correcting the draft of this book; Reverend Murdo Pollock and Mrs. Joyce Pollock for their compassionate comments and discussions about the book; Reverend Dr. James Young-Key Min, Cobden-Queen's Line Pastoral Charge, Cobden, Ontario, Canada, for sharing ideas and encouragement; Dr. Inge Russell, Mrs. In-Soon Choi, and Mr. David Caravan for their insightful suggestions. I also thank Reverend Sheldon Dyck, First Baptist Church, London, Ontario, who was kind enough to provide support for this project and made arrangements for a meeting with Mrs. Elsie Lunn; Reverend Daniel Dong-Won Lee for his encouraging foreword; Mr. Kwon I-Yong and Ms. Lee Mee-Hae in Seoul, Korea, for their assistance with the foreword. And last, but not least, many thanks are extended to the publisher and staff of Authentic/Paternoster, Colorado Springs, Colorado, USA. Thank you all. It is my prayer that this book will touch the hearts of all who read it.

Hoyeon Choi, PhD

It is often said that enthusiasm is infectious. That statement has proven true for me in assisting Dr. Hoyeon Choi with this translation of the exciting Korean language book, *My Cup Overflows*. Dr. Choi had been profoundly affected by reading this story of the life and witness of Mang Eui-Soon and sensed a calling to have this story translated from Korean to English to make it available to a whole new generation of readers. He has worked tirelessly and with a generosity of spirit to provide this vehicle by which English-language readers can discover this poignant, but heartbreaking story. It has been a privilege to assist in this project and to share Dr. Choi's enthusiasm for telling the story of how Mang Eui-Soon lived a life of service to others for the sake of Jesus Christ. In the midst of political, economic, and religious upheaval, he lived a life of meaning and purpose. Mang Eui-Soon's example of vibrant faith and willing service, and the enthusiastic response of his biographer Chung Yeun-Hee and translator Dr. Hoyeon Choi, can touch the lives of people in our own current time of global unrest and upheaval. It is my prayer that readers will become enthusiastic in their own desire and willingness to emulate Mang Eui-Soon's ability to lead through loving service to others.

Sincerely,
Rev. Gordon Timbers

FOREWORD

My Cup Overflows, the novel written by Chung Yeun-Hee, is based on a true story about a young man's struggle to live a life of meaning and purpose. It is the story of Mang Eui-Soon, who lived during the turbulent times of recent Korean history. The readers will also encounter Jesus Christ in this story because he was the master and inspiration of Mang Eui-Soon's life. The novel was initiated by the witness of Reverend Dr. Park Jae-Hoon (now retired) and by the writings of Chung Yeun-Hee, who described Mang's life as a "lily that blossomed in the barren soil of Korean churches" in that difficult time of civil war and anarchy. Through this novel, the fragrance of that lily still affects and enriches us today.

We are living in a time of material affluence and spiritual deficiency. We are longing for the same kind of overflowing spiritual power that sustained Mang Eui-Soon. My congratulations extend to Dr. Hoyeon Choi and Reverend Gordon Timbers, both from Canada, who dedicated their time and effort to complete this English-language edition.

I strongly believe that this book witnesses to the transforming power of Jesus Christ and will transmit that power beyond the constituency of Korean churches to the wider world to change people's lives.

The book will enlighten us to value those who lead by serving others rather than seeking to dominate others, following the example of Christ, kneeling at his disciples' feet with towel and washbasin. I wholeheartedly recommend this book to all of you.

Reverend Daniel Dong-Won Lee
A servant for Christ's kingdom
The Global Mission Church, Seoul, Korea

ABOUT THE AUTHOR

Chung Yeun-Hee was born in 1936 in Seoul, Korea, and earned a BA in Korean literature at Ewha Woman's University. In 1957, she made her writing debut with her short story *Paryusang*, winning the spring literature contest award from *Dong-A Il Bo* (daily news). She subsequently worked as a journalist at *Sae-Ke Il Bo* (daily news) and as a lecturer at her alma mater. In 1969 as a correspondent, she went on a world tour, writing a series of travel sketches for the *Kyunghyang Shinmun* (newspaper). In 1979, she was awarded a Korean Novelists' Association Award for her novel *Makchayo Makcha* (*It's a Last Bus)* and a Korean Literature Writers' Award in 1981 for her novel *Saramdeuleui doci* (*The City of the People)*. She won the Korea Literary Award for *Nanji Island* in 1984. She also won the Yun Dong-Ju Literary Award for *The Horn*. Chung has regularly written novels for a number of newspapers and literary journals, including *Hyundai Munhak* (*Modern Literature*) and *Munhak Sasang* (*Literary Thoughts*). A short story was translated into English and published in a Columbia University quarterly, *Translations*, and *Ainu Ainu*, a collection of short stories. Chung is currently publisher of *Letters to Housewives*, a monthly newsletter. She lives in Seoul and serves as president of the Korea Literary Women's Association.

INTRODUCTION
The Germination of a Seed

May 1983

By Chung Yeun-Hee

In 1981, one day at dusk, I received a phone call from a woman whose voice was calm and polite, asking for my home address, and then she forwarded a letter to me via local mail written by Dr. Park Jae-Hoon, a well-known hymn composer living in Toronto, Canada. With beautiful penmanship and clarity of thought, the letter expressed a compassionate patriotism for Korea that moved me greatly. Dr. Park indicated that an article of mine in the November issue of the *Journal of Christian Thought* had given him an idea for an opera he was planning to compose about the March Movement.[1] He then asked me to write a script for the opera. I considered this for some time but eventually gave it up as something beyond my competence. I

1. On March 1, 1919, there was a mass protest by Koreans against the repressive policies of the Japanese occupying forces. A "declaration of Korean independence" was read, and the people joined in a peaceful demonstration, asking for self-determination. The movement spread across the country, and even though these aspirations were expressed through demonstrations that were acts of nonviolence, some 7,500 Koreans were killed and 45,000 arrested. More than 100,000 people were wounded. Some of the Japanese rules were eventually relaxed, and the military police were replaced by a civilian force. Limited freedom of the press was permitted, but all of that changed back to repression when Japan entered World War II.

recommended Mrs. Kim Ja-Rim for this task and put them in contact with each other.

During Passion Week that year, I received another letter from Dr. Park, which contained four full pages of a personal recollection entitled *The Story of My Friend, Mang Eui-Soon*. The emotional impact of these pages brought me to my knees. I have met neither Dr. Park Jae-Hoon nor Mang Eui-Soon, who had died more than thirty years before. I first came to know of Mang Eui-Soon through this letter. But these two people helped me realize that a new shoot was emerging from my very soul. A tightly closed seed had been rolling about in a deep and dark place within me, and now it suddenly erupted, and a new consciousness burst forth that would lead me into new understandings of my faith and myself.

How to proceed with *The Story of My Friend, Mang Eui-Soon* remained constant in my heart throughout the spring and summer of 1981, and by late autumn, it had begun to take form. From late October on, I began to search out resource people still living, who might be able to tell me about him and his life. I met his stepmother, Kwonsa[2] La Chang-Seok, who had loved her stepson dearly, and Reverend Bae Myung-Joon, who had served the Namdaemun Church during the Korean War. In the course of searching for information about him, I heard of miracles that were beyond human comprehension. Through several sources of information, I was able to be in contact and meet with many people who were associated with Mang Eui-Soon. From them, I obtained many letters that he

2. This is a title given in most Protestant churches in Korea to women who dedicate themselves to a ministry of pastoral visitation and assisting church leaders. It is a counterpart to the role of a church elder.

had written. Some had been written during his early years as a prisoner of war and were faintly penciled on the back of used charts from the war camp hospital because writing paper and pencils were scarce. Among other letters received were eulogies written by his friends and tearful accounts from Chinese prisoners of war to whom he ministered.

In November I decided to start writing, but first I visited the site at Kojeri, Busan, where he had been imprisoned. When I completed this tour, I was extremely ill and groaned in pain for ten days. I had encountered the soul of Mang Eui-Soon, a man who had been endlessly lonely on earth, but who had transformed pain and distress into heavenly joy on his pilgrimage. I met many people during this time who loved this man. He was still joyfully alive to them. For them, he was like starlight breaking through the dark storm clouds of the Korean War. His light still shines, his life an example that the power of love enables us to transform distress and suffering into abundant life.

A Brief History of Korea

Korea knew little about the Western world until Korean envoys to Beijing brought home maps of Europe and books on Catholicism during the seventeenth century. Dutch navigators drifting into the southern shore of Cheju Island were rescued and employed in the king's court. One of them, Hendrik Hamel, returned to Amsterdam and in 1668 published his story of adventures, and Korea was introduced to Western countries. Korea has enjoyed five thousand years of vibrant history and unique culture. The first recorded history started with the three kingdoms of the Korean Peninsula in the first century. On the peninsula, Korea was an independent and united country for twelve hundred years.

In its prime, one of the kingdoms, Goguryeo, ruled Manchuria to the north as well as one-half of the peninsula to the south. For much of the time, the Korean Choson kingdom closed doors to most countries except for China and earned the name "Hermit Kingdom." After Japan completed the Meiji Restoration under the influence of the West, Korea began to open its borders. The superpowers around the world were expanding and making colonies to secure raw materials and markets. There were desperate efforts by Korean politicians to modernize the country, some relying on China, others on Japan or Russia, but all failed. Government corruption and ineptitude, along with the influx of foreign powers, accelerated the fall of the last kingdom, and Korea became an arena of the world powers vying for power: China, Japan, Russia, and the United States. After Japan won the war with China and Russia, it blatantly annexed Korea for thirty-six years (1910–1945) and waged war with the United States. Japan used Korea as a bullet shield and exploited natural and human resources for war supplies.

As World War II neared its end, the world leaders of the Allied powers met at Potsdam and Yalta regarding the fate of Korea after Japan lost, and Korea was put under the trusteeship of international powers: the United States, the United Kingdom, China, and the Soviet Union. Just a few months before the surrender of Japan, Americans had proposed to Russia that Korea be divided along the thirty-eighth parallel in order to demilitarize the Japanese armies in Korea. The division has been in place ever since. Between the years 1945 and 1950, prior to the Korean War, right- and left-wing leaders engaged in extreme confrontation to try to control the hegemony of political power backed up by the United States and Russia.

Communism had spread throughout Asia by 1950. Red China completed the revolution by expelling Chiang Kai-Shek's government to Formosa. Russia spearheaded a national campaign of bullying in Eastern Europe and Korea. The Korean Peninsula became an arena for the ideological strife called "the Cold War." The early Communist movement in Korea was not directly affiliated or connected to other Communist regimes. Its initial motivation was to fight against the occupation of Korea by Japan and to bring about Korean independence. As this struggle continued, the Korean resistance looked for help from outside sources. Japanese repression forced it to go into exile and to look to China and the Soviet Union for support. Some of these exiled Koreans fought the Japanese military as guerrillas across Manchuria as part of the Chinese Communist People's Liberation Army.

In Korea, strife soon developed between those who were pro-Communist and those who were pro-American. Some collaborators who worked for Japan under its occupation later found employment with the provisional American government in Korea (under Hodge) and with the subsequent government of Rhee Syngman. Many of the pro-Communist nationalists who had fought against Japan had suffered hardships in the struggle for independence and felt they had been sidelined.

While Americans established a capitalist, pro-American government named the Republic of Korea (ROK) in South

Korea, Russians helped North Korea to enable Kim Il-Sung to establish a Communist, pro-Soviet government called the Democratic People's Republic Korea (DPRK). Korean leaders tried hard to unify the country but failed because of internal strife and external interference. In the South under the supervision of the United Nations, a general election was held, and the government was established three years later on August 15, 1948. The Soviets assisted North Korea to build up military hardware, and on June 25, 1950, North Korea invaded South Korea. With blitzkrieg tactics, the North Korean troops thrust down the peninsula near Busan and its surrounding areas (Nakdong River perimeter). With the intervention of the UN forces, of which 80 percent were American, General Douglas A. MacArthur launched an amphibious assault on Inchon in September 1950 and pushed the North Korean troops back to Yaru River. At this point the Chinese army intervened, and the UN forces retreated to near the thirty-eighth parallel. The war settled into a stalemate, and an armistice agreement was signed in July 1953, ending with the demarcation line similar to that of the prewar state. Casualties from the war were very high, with 273,000 Koreans dead from North and South Korea, 37,000 US soldiers dead, 3,000 UN forces dead (excluding Americans), and the destruction of infrastructure and dislocation of Koreans. Ironically the Korean War is not yet over; the war in the divided country is just pausing.

POLITICAL FIGURES AND INDIVIDUAL NAMES APPEARING IN THIS BOOK

Political Figures (see also notes)

Ahn Jae-Hong (1891–1965). A key member of the Committee for the Preparation of Korean Independence (CPKI) to rebuild the country and a chief civil administrator, 1947–1948.

Arnold, Archibald V. (1889–1973). Major general, the first governor-general of South Korea under US Army Military Government in Korea (USAMGIK), 1945.

Chiang Kai-Shek (1887–1975). A Chinese military and political leader. Chiang attempted to eradicate the Chinese Communists but ultimately failed, forcing his government to retreat to Taiwan, where he continued serving as the director-general.

Cho Man-Shik (1882–1959?). A devoted Christian political leader, called a Gandhi of Korea, formed the North Korean Democratic Party, visited North Korea for the unification of Korea, but did not return.

Hodge, John Reed (1893–1963). Lieutenant general, US commander in chief, US Twenty-fourth Corps Tenth Army, military governor under USAMGIK, 1945–1948. He took his corps of the US Tenth Army to Korea under order of General MacArthur landing at Inchon on September 8, 1945. He was a commanding officer receiving the surrender of all Japanese troops in Korea south of the thirty-eighth parallel.

Kim Ku (1876–1949). One of the most honored political leaders in Korea, and in 1931, he organized a nationalist group to liberate Korea from Japan. Kim was the president of the provisional government of Korea in Shanghai in 1927. Kim was assassinated in 1949.

Kim Kyu-Shik (1881–1950). A political leader and chairman of the Interim Legislative Assembly in South Korea, 1946–1948.

Rhee Syngman (1885–1965). A political leader and president of South Korea, 1948–1960.

Song Chin-Woo (1889–1945). A general manager of the Korea Democratic Party (KDP), working for USAMGIK. Song was assassinated.

Yeo Un-Hyong (1886–1947). A national figure, patriot, the chairman of the People's Labor Party, and chairman of the Provisional Council in 1945. Yeo was assassinated.

Individuals Associated with Mang Eui-Soon

Bae Myung-Joon. A minister in charge of the Namdaemun Church when Mang Eui-Soon attended.

Bae Sook-Kyung. A female classmate at Choson Seminary.

Chang Hyung-Jin. A friend of Mang Eui-Soon.

Kang Hui-Dong. POW and a member of the wilderness church in the camp.

Kim Young-Joo. A friend and university classmate of Mang Eui-Soon.

La Chang-Seok. Mang Eui-Soon's stepmother.

Lee Hoe-Jin. POW and a member of the wilderness church in the camp.

Lee Sung-Soo. A senior student of Choson Seminary.

Lee Won-Shik. POW and a member of the wilderness church in the camp.

Mang Kwan-Ho. Mang Eui-Soon's father, kidnapped to North Korea.

Moon Myung-Churl. POW and a member of the wilderness church in the camp.

Myung Hyung-Churl. Joined the group when Mang Eui-Soon fled to South Korea.

Yu Chung-In. Army captain, a female friend of Mang Eui-Soon.

In this translation of the true story of Mang Eui-Soon, some names were changed to protect the identities of certain characters.

Mang Eui-Soon's Escape Route to the South

PART ONE
A Seed Takes Root

Unfailing Legacy

My name is Chang Hyung-Jin, a friend of Mang Eui-Soon. Mang is remembered as a flower in full blossom that will not wither. He carried his name for twenty-six years and eight months while living in this world. His name may seem strange and banal to those who did not know him, but it still evokes a sense of community for those who knew him or who were associated with him. To me his name means a shining and guiding star. It cannot be compared to any temporal wealth or honors. To call him by his three-word name[1] is still insufficient and incomplete. His legacy is more than a name, Mang Eui-Soon—like clothes that still carry the warmth of the body that wore them.

In departing from this world and leaving his name behind, he left an immortal spirit with which we can identify. Through even the mention of his name, we can recollect his life and character and appreciate the true identity of the human being

1. Most Korean names consist of three words, although some have two words and others four words. The first word is the last name, and the next two are the first name, with no middle name.

who faced deep sorrow with the inherent limitation and vulnerability of mortality, but with an eternal spirit. His name inspires us to embrace an eternity with a profound sense of indwelling comfort and hope.

A Kendo Incident

I first met Mang Eui-Soon at the Pyongyang Secondary School in 1940.[2] Although we were classmates, I did not take much notice of him at first because he didn't stand out in class or at recess. It was nearly a year later during our kendo[3] class that the Japanese kendo teacher warned Mang several times that he was not showing any enthusiasm for the class. Mang was neither shorter nor weaker than his classmates, but all kendo equipment seemed cumbersome to him: the round bamboo stick made up of four pieces of bamboo, the face mask, the shield to protect the chest and stomach, the woven long-sleeved gloves, and the headpiece to protect the neck; he wanted to throw it all away. The teacher blasted him, "If you don't behave yourself now, I will challenge you." Calling for such a sparring match from a teacher meant an outright attack on the student, and ominous thoughts flashed into my mind. Despite stern warnings, Mang Eui-Soon seemed nonchalant.

If the teacher found the student unsatisfactory, he would declare a match against him and order the student to attack him first. If the student resisted, he would lash out at him

---

2. The educational, political, and economic systems were entirely under Japanese control.
3. Kendo is a form of fencing and is a component of Japanese martial arts.

ruthlessly. Once the student started to defend himself, the teacher's anger was already aflame. Even if the student's face was bruised and streaked with tears under the mask, the beating would not stop until the teacher's madness had died out.

The beating went on longer and seemed harsher than any previous punishments. Yet, from the beginning, Mang Eui-Soon did not intend to defend himself. The teacher interpreted this act of nonresistance as though Mang considered the kendo uniform itself disgraceful to him. Even when the teacher was panting with the effort, Mang Eui-Soon still showed no emotion.

The teacher shrieked, "Tell me why you dare not do your best even though you can!" But Mang kept silent. The teacher gasped and cried out, "You are deliberately shunning kendo. Why?" Mang said nothing.

When it was over, his face was horribly disfigured. The teacher had whipped him using a leather slipper taken from the sole of a Japanese army boot. He turned his swollen face toward me and smiled gently. I saw a marvelous peace in him. This was his potential power. Despite beatings and pain, his spirit glowed brilliantly.

On our way home, he did not speak much, and we parted company at the crossroads. It was several days later, again on our way home from school, that I said, "I've thought about what happened at our last kendo class. Tomorrow we will have class again. How do you feel about it?"

"They call it discipline," he said, "but that is not what it is. It is an impediment in our way of searching for a new direction. I am dismayed by the stupidity of it all and our helpless acceptance of it."

"But we don't have a choice," I retorted. "What will you do in the future?"

"I will not pursue a cowardly path," he responded.

Japan occupied Korea from 1910 to 1945, engaging in war throughout the Pacific region.[4] To promote the war effort across the country, it forced military training upon all schoolchildren. The Japanese teachers shaved their heads to make their appearance more menacing. They often gave us group punishment, disguising it as "mental rearmament," designed to toughen us up.

The physical punishment started again when the teacher became annoyed because we did not grab rifles quickly. He beat us on our buttocks while we were in the pushup position. He then made us march in the squat position for a long period of time. Even though we were exhausted from the marching and bruised and swollen from the beatings, Mang Eui-Soon did not flinch. I glanced at him and saw that he radiated a marvelous power I had never seen before.

Our punishment ended at dusk, and I went to Mang Eui-Soon. "You stood up well today."

He responded with a smile. "I was lucky today to have a mild punishment."

But when he pulled up his pant leg and I saw that his legs had been beaten by wooden sticks and the skin was broken and bloodied, I was shocked.

---

4. Japan launched a surprise attack on Pearl Harbor, Hawaii, on December 7, 1941. In response, the United States declared war on Japan and became a combatant in the Second World War.

After pulling down his pant leg and putting on his gaiters, he said, "It could have been worse. Even if you flinch from hurts, it will not help pain."

"Pain is still pain," I replied.

While I kept pressing him with questions, he got dressed. Finally he said, "When we grow up, we will see more pain than this. We are getting good training for the future."

I was quite at a loss as to what to say. I was suspicious of his motivation because I thought he was hiding his feelings by being cunning, showing his hidden heroism. He finished dressing and got up quickly, saying nothing further. He waited until I had finished getting dressed and took hold of my hand to help me up. Then he offered some earnest responses to my questions.

"My hatred of the Japanese is so intense that it has given me the strength to overcome my pain. I contemplated the meaning of suffering as I experienced this hatred, and the more I concentrated on the suffering, the better I was able to overcome the pain." He was so serious and firm in what he was saying that I could make no response.

It was getting dark by this time, and he stood in the corner of the schoolyard like an evergreen tree growing tall, despite suffering. After the kendo incident and group punishment, everyone avoided him.

It was not until the next spring that he came to my attention again. A few Japanese teachers had conspired together to find some fault against him. When they found him teaching a Korean Bible class in Sunday school, they seized on the opportunity to punish him. They beat him to a pulp. When he returned to the classroom, a few friends were waiting for him, packing his schoolbag. Seeing him they were terrified and extremely agitated.

"**** Japanese. Wipe out the ********," they said. Along with my friends, I stood there with my fists clenched and my whole body shaking.

"How long do we have to suffer these insults?" I cried in frustration. Mang Eui-Soon, picking up his schoolbag, said quietly, "I am sorry."

"What do you mean by that?" I asked. "Do you think that we are being harassed because of you? You are talking foolishness. This is not just about harassment. This is our country at stake. We should take revenge upon the Japanese."

Mang Eui-Soon continued to talk quietly. "We were just beaten and abused. With our afflictions, we will take revenge." Tears welled up from his bruised eyes as we challenged his nonsense. How could our suffering be a way of taking revenge?

"By beating us viciously, their days become numbered. We should be thankful and comforted."

In response to our challenge, Mang Eui-Soon stressed that our comfort would come from God. This provoked a fierce argument from me. I called him a hypocrite and stupid, but he only cautioned us to stop what we were saying.

One by one, we dispersed and walked to the schoolyard gate. When we were some distance away from the school, I approached Mang Eui-Soon, who was striding along as if nothing had happened to him. I asked him what he would do now about his involvement with the Sunday school. He declared that he would quit.

"Is this because of the harassment?" I asked.

He replied that he could put up with being beaten, but he feared that his minister might be thrown into prison. The Japanese had been spying on any religious activities other than their own Shinto form of worship, which promoted Japanese nationalism. We had surrendered to their military invasion, but they continued to beat us down. Mang Eui-Soon was distressed about the possibility that his minister might be put into prison and that his own actions could be responsible for such a punishment.

"Don't you hate them?"

Mang Eui-Soon answered, "I am a sinner too. I have no right to hate them."

"Did you pray to God for this insight?" I asked sarcastically.

But Mang Eui-Soon answered my question faithfully. "Yes," he said, "I prayed while I was being beaten up. I thanked God that I was not in a position to harm them. I prayed that I would gain the insight that God would forgive them and save them."

This seemed complete nonsense to me, and I asked him if he were mocking our anger with his sophisticated arguments. He responded to this challenge by gazing up into the night sky. His face was torn, but he was not at all ugly. I wondered why he was gazing up with such rapt attention.

He turned to me and said, "We should have indignation; we need social justice. This is an indispensable requirement for life in this world. God works to eliminate these evils so that we can understand his will and follow him. Without this, we cannot achieve peace."

"Who are we to follow? Who is 'he'?" I asked Mang Eui-Soon.

"His name is Jesus."

I said nothing because his answer seemed so strange and absurd. When I got home, I could not go to sleep and spent most of the night awake, thinking. One part of me was engulfed by my hatred of the Japanese, a feeling that flared up like flames in a furnace. Another part of me was afflicted by my inability to believe in the possibility of peace. But when I thought calmly about Mang Eui-Soon and how he had stared at the night sky, my anger dissolved, and I felt a sense of comfort and assurance. It was indeed possible that I could be free of hatred. It was a strange and mysterious phenomenon.

Mang Eui-Soon, who had never seemed to me to be outstanding in any other way, was transformed through his sufferings into a person with a powerful charisma. That night I felt that I was approaching an understanding that still eluded me. Mang Eui-Soon possessed something quite different, something that other people did not. Finally, near dawn, I fell asleep with the image of Mang Eui-Soon's face in my mind.

The next day he came to school with a disfigured face. His classmates were agitated at seeing this and wanted to know what had happened to him, but he himself was calm, as if nothing had happened. I felt myself drawn to him like a magnet.

"Can you stand the pain?" I asked. "Your face looks so bad."

He smiled in response, and as he smiled, I felt the pain of his scars. "If you know that this is not my real face, then that's all right." He gave me an affectionate glance that touched my heart. Tears welled up in my eyes. Mang Eui-Soon went on to say that each man has his own true face. "What we see and experience is not everything. I may look disgusting now, but my real face is intact. So it is with everyone. Beatings, hatred, exploitation, and revenge are not everything. It is important to believe that what we see is not all there is."

After a moment, he asked me if I had trouble sleeping the night before.

"How did you know?" I asked.

"I was with you."

I took in a deep breath of air and clearly saw marks engraved on the life and person of Mang Eui-Soon. Who gave him these marks? What do they mean? What is the power that underlies his suffering and distress? These questions stirred me greatly.

Piano Performance

Soon after this incident I went with Mang Eui-Soon to his church. I was amazed as I watched him: his skillfulness in playing the piano, his singing voice when he taught hymns to the children, and his posture when he sang. As I listened to the songs, I felt joy and freedom from my hatred and revenge toward the Japanese and the uncertainty about my future. I saw him, not as a seventeen-year-old boy anymore, nor as an adult, either. I saw something in him, a presence from which emanated a peace.

"Your piano performance is wonderful! I never imagined that you were a musician," I told him afterward. He smiled and told me that he had enjoyed my piano practicing at school. I was pleased—I had not known he had paid attention to my piano sessions. Having no piano in my house, I had to wait my turn to use the piano at school. I asked Mang Eui-Soon why he didn't play at school, given that he had such a fine ability.

When he protested that his playing was not good enough to show others at school, I commented that from what I had just heard, he must have been practicing for some time.

"We have a piano in my house," he said. "My sister majored in piano. I learned to play by watching over her shoulder. She was married last year. These days, when I play the piano, I think of her."

I was discovering new things about him and his family. The Japanese war propaganda claimed their victory on all fronts, and food, clothing, and other commodities were extremely scarce. Koreans lived in poverty and had to accept this as their fate. Less than 10 percent of the population had enough to eat. Sending a daughter to college to study piano at such a time revealed his family's wealth. Sometime later I was surprised to find out that he was the son of Elder Mang Kwan-Ho, a well-known pillar of the Changdaeche Church and, perhaps, the wealthiest man in Pyongyang City. But Mang Eui-Soon was unassuming and lived a very simple life. His mother was as cheerful as his father was solemn. Mang Eui-Soon had a married sister, an older brother attending a junior college, and a younger sister. Peacefulness surrounded his family.

I frequently visited his home, and music brought us close, but I much preferred listening to his playing than playing myself. He was a fountain of music, and his music illuminated his very soul. His singing projected a message of peace. I learned new selections of Beethoven, Mozart, and Schumann from him.

While he was playing the piano, Mang's clear eyes shimmered. "Chopin was sentimental, except in his polonaises," he told me. "He had a majestic patriotism, while exhibiting a subtlety and elegance, and to play polonaises requires a mastery of performance techniques. Thinking of his fatherland, of Poland, Chopin grieved over the occupation of his country by the Russians, and his soul glowed through his music." When Mang Eui-Soon was playing a polonaise, he was not a boy, but a giant, carrying an immense sorrow.

A similar thing happened when he played Schumann or when he sang "Wanderer" or "Winter's Journey." He sank into the solitude and sorrow of Schumann's poetry and music. When he sang Schubert or Gounod's "Ave Maria," he assumed a solemn piety and posture of prayer.

When we were together, we felt no sense of the anger, hatred, or anguish inflicted by Japanese teachers. This world belonged to us. This amazing and beautiful time during my boyhood became a secure fortress that offered an undisturbed peace.

But just over the wall from our fortress, pain and despair were lurking, waiting to devour our peace. Mang Eui-Soon's married sister died during our last school year. His love for her was intense. "My sister is my music. She is the fountain of my songs," he had told me. I wept with him.

One day when his parents were out, he played Mozart's Rondo in A Major. It was like new sprouts pushing through the earth toward the sun. I can remember the music: Köchel no. 512 in A Major. The music expressed something beginning to bloom like a shy moss rose, a yearning of joy and also a rising sorrow. The rhythm of the music was a wailing more profound than any crying.

"This music is my sister. This is the sound of her music. I have wanted to play this piece of music so much, but I haven't been able to because it would affect my parents too much." He repeated the piece from the beginning, his face wet with tears. At that moment I realized for the first time that we should accept the grief we feel when we are parted from the people we love.

A few months later we heard that his brother, who had been conscripted into the Japanese army while still a student, had been killed in battle. I wondered then what the pain threshold would be for Mang Eui-Soon. No one could begin to fathom the depths of his suffering. Yet he came to school as before. He calmly attended "the labor mobilization" through which Japanese authorities forced students to join the labor force, using various reasons and excuses as Japan neared the end of the war.

I could not offer him any words of condolence. For a while I did not even visit him. I could not summon up enough courage to face his parents. He was as warm and calm as ever, and I could only imagine the weight of pain and misery that had to be racking him. I could see that a spark had been lit within him that had its own flame. He had an unexpected aura about him, a sign of the fire that was building deep inside.

Korea Divided

We graduated from the school at the time of Korea's liberation from Japan.[5] But while everyone celebrated the liberation of the country, Mang Eui-Soon suddenly disappeared. When he reappeared, I asked him where he had been. He just smiled, so I continued to question him, accusing him of acting as if he were not Korean and even challenging him to admit that his personal tragedies were suppressing his ability to feel joy at the liberation. I was upset because we were not sharing the joy of freedom together.

He looked up at me and said very slowly, "Now this country will begin to suffer. The Yalta Conference[6] signed last February was a bad omen for Korea. And the Potsdam Declaration[7] will be toxic to Korea's future. We will soon leave Pyongyang."

I wondered what he meant. Was he planning to leave? I believed that he was wrong. I was hot blooded in my youth, and the joy of liberation was too exciting to see it as bad news for our country. He was being too pessimistic about our nation's future.

5. Korea gained independence on August 15, 1945, when Japan was defeated in the Second World War.
6. The Yalta Conference took place on February 4, 1945, in Crimea (Yalta). The heads of the Allied governments met together to discuss issues arising from the defeat of the Axis nations in the Second World War. It was determined that Korea would be put under the trusteeship of international powers (the United States, the United Kingdom, and Soviet Union) for a significant period of time (twenty to thirty years). The Soviet Union secretly agreed to enter the war against Japan within three months of Germany's surrender and was promised Sakhalin, the Kuril Islands, and an occupation zone in Korea.
7. On July 17, 1945, the Allied forces met to clarify and implement agreements previously reached at the Yalta Conference. This declaration reconfirmed the plan to put Korea under an international trusteeship.

But soon we were making plans to leave Pyongyang to go south of the thirty-eighth parallel, the dividing line between South and North. The Russian army had already landed in North Korea, and some fighting had broken out.

The US Twenty-fourth Corps landed in South Korea under the leadership of Lieutenant General John R. Hodge, and on September 8, 1945, it was announced that South Korea would be under his military rule, and three days later, Major General A. V. Arnold was appointed as military governor to take political control.

Two days before the Americans landed in South Korea, a pro-Communist government formed to seize power by taking advantage of the vacuum of the politics. They put up a sign declaring themselves the Committee for the Preparation of Korean Independence (CPKI). They selected fifty-five representatives on September 14, 1945, and announced the formation of the Korea People's Republic (KPR).[8] These Communists held meetings every day and announced the names of their cabinet ministers. With lightning speed, they plastered the country with red posters. The political parties on the right felt a great uneasiness about the provocative actions of those on the left. Later many political factions of both the pro-Communist and anti-Communist split and engaged in acrimonious fighting, and this accelerated political instability and contributed to solidifying the permanent national division.

8. An opposing view insists that the KPR government represented the full political spectrum of Koreans: it included anti-Communist groups, Communists, and leftists. This was a genuine attempt to create a popular coalition government but was short lived because the US-led provisional government (under Hodge) refused to recognize it. The KPR was founded by Yeo Un-Hyong, a popular nationalist and cofounder of the Korean Provisional Government (KPG).

The Korean Peninsula was like a simmering pot into which anything and everything was thrown whether it was beneficial or not. Everyone rushed toward the kettle, but no one was yet in possession of it. The contents splashed out and spilled over in all directions. Some got burned and others got hurt in the crush, and everyone blamed someone else. Oh, what a wretched country, already stomped over repeatedly, brutalized, and occupied by stronger neighbors[9]—plus blood feuds! It was as if the shame of the country was laid bare and its nakedness uncovered because of the arrogant behavior of the people in not recognizing their own accountability.

Desperate and brutal fighting broke out, and everyone claimed ownership of the bread called "freedom" being offered by other countries, and each prevented the other from taking it. The spirit of liberation turned into a shambles, and the joy of freedom turned into battle. There seemed to be no one who thought about the future of the country with patriotic fervor and an open heart. Everyone attempted to stand up and wield force. No one was willing to listen to anyone else. Numerous political parties and social groups ebbed and flowed, and among them, the Communists, with their international network and experience, were most active.

We had to leave for the South, which was by that time a powder keg ready to explode. We promised to meet again in Seoul and left separately to reach safe ground. It was early

9. Because of Korea's proximity to mainland China and Japan, it suffered innumerable invasions from these countries throughout its history. Some notable invasions took place in the seventh and seventeenth centuries by China (Sui, Tang, and Quing), in the thirteenth century by the Mongols, and in the sixteenth and early twentieth centuries by Japan.

December when I arrived in Seoul. Rhee Syngman,[10] who had fought for Korean independence, had returned from Hawaii on October 16, 1945; and shortly after this, on November 23, a group of prominent nationalists of the Korean Provisional Government (KPG)[11] arrived from Shanghai. These included Kim Ku[12] and Kim Kyu-Shik.[13] The political situation was becoming more complicated, and conflict was imminent.

Then from the resolutions adopted in the Moscow Conference of Foreign Ministers[14] in December 1945 in Moscow, the United States, Russia, and Great Britain declared

---

10. Rhee lived in exile for many years in America while working for Korean independence. He became the first elected president of South Korea (1948–1960) but remains a controversial figure. He was a strong anti-Communist but used harsh tactics to eliminate his political opponents. His presidency ended in resignation because of charges of illegal election activities. Some conservative circles still regard him as a founder of the nation, but others consider him a sinister and dangerous political leader.

11. On April 13, 1919, ten Korean leaders in exile came together in Shanghai to establish the Korean Provisional Government (KPG). Their aim was to coordinate a systematic and efficient resistance against Japan. This promoted the demand for Korean independence and imbued this movement with an underlying ideology and philosophy.

12. Kim spent his entire life working for Korean independence and is still revered by many Koreans as a patriotic nationalist. He served as a president of the Korean Provisional Government (KPG). He organized a Korea Patriotic Legion to replace the Japanese army and political leadership. He also established the Korean Liberation Army to fight against Japan. Because of his strong objection to the international trusteeship and the division of the country, he was not favored by the US-sponsored provisional government led by Hodge. In 1949, Kim was assassinated by Ahn Doo-Whi, which suggested the involvement of a right-wing conspiracy either by Rhee or the CIA, but no details of such conspiracies have ever been revealed.

13. Kim was a leading member of the KPG along with Kim Ku. Kim opposed the South Korean election of 1948 because of the nonparticipation of the North. After his failed efforts to broker reunification, he retired from politics.

14. This conference called for Korea to be put under an international trusteeship for a defined maximum period of five years. A meeting was convened and attended by the foreign ministers of the United States, Great Britain, and Russia to discuss issues raised by the end of the war. They reconfirmed the agreement on Korean issues made in the earlier Yalta Conference and Potsdam Declaration.

that Korea was to become the object of an international trusteeship for five years. This trusteeship proposal outraged many Koreans.

The Korea Democratic Party (KDP),[15] since it was associated with the US military government, took control of politics and finances by supporting Rhee Syngman as its leader. This did not allow any room for nationalist Kim Ku and the Korean Provisional Government (KPG). In the beginning, the Communists opposed the trusteeship, but they changed suddenly because Russia was part of the trusteeship.

I met Mang Eui-Soon in Seoul in January 1946 as extreme cold was sweeping through the city. People were panic stricken when they heard that the general manager of the KDP, Song Chin-Woo, working for the American military government, had been assassinated in his home. The entire country was gripped by fear that more assassins would go on the rampage through the country. We were chilled to the bone and felt that our country was rushing headlong into disaster. We had no one to turn to and no place to go. We were completely confused.

Mang Eui-Soon's family arrived in Seoul empty-handed. Fortunately, they found a friend who attended Namdaemun Church and stayed in his house, but the future was grim for them.

"I am so thankful to see that both of us are still alive," I said to Mang Eui-Soon when we were finally able to meet

15. On September 4, 1945, the right-wing conservative leaders formed a new political party, the Korea Democratic Party (KDP), which supported the KPG. This party combined many small parties, such as the Korea Democratic Party, Choson National Party, and Korea National Party. On January 26, 1949, the KDP was dissolved, and a new party, the Democratic National Party, was formed.

again. At first he and I just shared the joy of reunion, but a few days later I grew worried about his future and that of his family. "What has happened to you and your family?"

"We found someone who was moving luggage across the border, a professional mover. We entrusted our luggage to him. We paid in advance as a token of appreciation because it was dangerous to go across the thirty-eighth parallel even without luggage. At the designated time and place, we waited for him, but he did not show up."

"Oh no," I said to him, dismayed. "You left the luggage with him and walked off? You should have kept your valuables aside," I said. "Oh, how naive your father and you are!"

"Well, our possessions did not just disappear. It is very likely that someone is using them now. He probably didn't cheat us on purpose. You must understand how dangerous it is just trying to cross the border without carrying anything. We are not as desperate as many other people. My father found someone from his hometown who owed him money, and he has promised to pay it back."

After Mang Eui-Soon and I talked about how we would catch up on our studies, I began to argue about the need for ambitious leaders to secure the future of our country—patriotic politicians and businessmen to build economic development and lawyers and judges to implement justice.

My friend listened to me very attentively and seriously until I finished. When I stopped, he disagreed. "Don't misunderstand me," he said. "I don't mean that your ideas are wrong. But I must serve someone else. It is extremely important for us to have good politicians and to live decent lives. But if our soul is not right in this life, we cannot find any meaning in anything. I have to live as a servant to the Lord. I think this is the only way people should live on this earth."

"Are you saying that only by faith can we govern ourselves rightly?" I asked.

"Yes, I am. And it is possible if only those who believe in the Lord are faithful unto death."

Several days later he brought me a book, *The Imitation of Christ*[16] by Thomas à Kempis. It had the subtitle *A Christian's Holy Standards*. Old, with frayed pages, it appeared difficult and didn't appeal to me.

"It may take you awhile to read it through," he said. "Pray while you read. Starting today, I will also pray for you while you read."

After this word from my friend, I could not help but read. Meditating before opening the book, I thought of the author, Thomas à Kempis, who was born in 1380 at Kempen near Düsseldorf and who had lived humbly for ninety-one years, dedicating himself only to God, and I thought of Mang Eui-Soon's peaceful face and his crystal clear eyes. I found myself compelled to kneel down when I considered the hundreds of faithful people who had been inspired by this book over the last five hundred years.

> Everyone naturally desires knowledge but of what use is knowledge itself without the fear of God? A humble countryman who serves God is more pleasing to Him

16. Written by Thomas à Kempis, translated and with an introduction by Leo Sherley-Price. Penguin Books, 1952.

> than a conceited intellectual who knows the course of the star but neglects his own soul.[17]

The secrets contained in this book opened up my soul. Considering the size of the book, I estimated I could finish it in a day, but as I began to read, I discovered that I could not read more than twenty pages in a night. I soon realized that it would be impossible for me to truly comprehend it in my lifetime even if I immersed myself in it continuously. The book was not meant for entertainment. It inflicted a new, unsettling agony within me.

I had aspired to establish myself in my country, to build a foundation, a place to erect a framework for success. I could not abandon the idea of being a successful man. The direction I planned to pursue was not the same direction Mang Eui-Soon had taken. The path he had chosen did not appeal to me, being too dull and bland. Even though I liked him dearly, I did not want to take the same path. But while reading the book, I was overtaken by a sense of shame and pain. I went to see Mang Eui-Soon, and we spent that whole spring on readings and prayers.

Hostility and strife overtook the political landscape. Although all parties insisted that they were true patriots, their goals seemed to be quite different. A joint committee of the United States and Russia was formed to establish a provisional Korean government. Parties that were favored either by the United States or Russia were formed, but they were divided over the process of establishing a Korean government and what form this government would take. One major point of

---

17. Ibid., chapter two, "On Personal Humility," p. 28. Used by permission.

agreement lay in their refusal to allow any Communists to be part of it and in establishing a government consisting only of Koreans.

Rhee Syngman insisted that, without establishing a single government run solely by South Korea, he could not, in principle, resolve anything, while Kim Ku proposed to resolve the dispute by bringing South and North Korea to the bargaining table. Kim Kyu-Shik demanded a joint government of South and North Koreans.

Both Kim Ku and Kim Kyu-Shik wanted the peaceful unification of the country and urged that national unity should not be disrupted under any circumstances. However, they were too naive to fathom the treacherous schemes of the Russians. Rhee Syngman revealed his lack of understanding of the international situation when he insisted on establishing a single government represented solely by South Koreans. He had learned that Yeo Un-Hyong[18] and Ahn Jae-Hong were preparing the CPKI to rebuild the country, and he was so uneasy about the development of local politics that he made the sudden decision to return home from his exile in the United States.

Mang Eui-Soon was disappointed with Rhee Syngman's refusal to work with other parties. "A grand national unity can only be achieved by serving each other," he moaned. We were

---

18. Yeo was a nationalist who formed the Committee for the Preparation of Korean Independence (CPKI) and a founding member of the Korean People's Party (KPP). He is revered in South and North Korea. He was a journalist, and his ideal was for a unified Korea represented by parties on the political right and left. Because of his centrist political position, he was attacked by the extremists on both sides. He was assassinated by Han Chi-Geun, a nineteen-year-old refugee from North Korea and an active member of a right-wing group.

sitting under a cherry tree near the creek; the water was flowing down the valley through Samchung Park. Looking at the woods and sky, he said, "The spring is so beautiful, but people don't appreciate it. This fighting has to come to an end!"

"Do you have any idea how to stop this bloody slaughter?"

He quietly gazed at my face and whispered, "The Bible tells us that if we had ten righteous people within the city, then the slaughter could be spared."

Peace on Campus

At the beginning of the fall semester at the university, Mang Eui-Soon registered in theological studies, and I registered in the religious music program. Because of the chaotic political circumstances, people were agitated, their opinions divided. There was very little tolerance toward others. Students were easily swayed from supporting one movement to another, and neither ideals nor professors could control them.

For a time things were quiet, but in October, news of a riot and mass slaughter in Daegu swept the whole nation. It originated in a strike by the members of the railway workers' union. Once the strike started, a left-wing group convinced forty other factories in Daegu to join the strike in sympathy.

On the night of October 1, thousands of laborers joined street demonstrations, singing the Communist anthem and advancing upon the hundreds of armed police officers who guarded the Daegu railway station. An unexpected blank shot fired by an armed policeman tore through the dark sky. Using that as a pretext, the crowds spread out and abruptly turned the area into a hell of stabbing, shooting, and killing.

Fear and dread overtook the city. The Communists agitated the people, rapidly spreading rumors. Unaware of the truth, people were stirred up; emotions fed emotions like oil on flames, and Daegu citizens rampaged through the streets and joined the demonstration. The riot broke out at eleven o'clock in the morning on October 2. The police attempted to disperse the demonstrators, but the mob swarmed the police, who panicked as the number of injured colleagues grew, and they fired wildly into the crowd. The police station was soon occupied by hundreds of students, and the homes of the policemen and their family members were attacked or captured and their possessions and furniture stolen.

The mobs were organized and swiftly mobilized to destroy communication devices, spread propaganda flyers, put up posters, and capture vehicles. The rioters drove the captured vehicles while singing the Communist anthem. They also set out to smash the homes of government officials.

In one day, the riot claimed the life of the chief investigator and many other officers and policemen at the Daegu police station and surrounding areas. The seriously injured policemen were taken to the hospitals, but the hospitals responded that unless the police stopped shooting, they would not admit them for treatment.

That evening the US Army was mobilized along with provincial police forces, and the riot was subdued. The place of the slaughter in downtown Daegu looked like a devastated battlefield. Twenty police officers had been killed, fifty had been wounded, and thirty were missing. Statistics for rioters and civilians were not available.

The riot did not stop there. It spread to Dalseong County. Rioters captured the police chief, the chief of the township office, and clerks in a police station and set the station on fire. The riot put the Young Nam area into a state of lawlessness.

Hearing the news, we were speechless. We lost any motivation for studying. Why had things gotten so ugly? How could our own people do such things? Was this the direction we would pursue after thirty-six years of shame under Japanese rule? Before one outbreak of violence could be fully investigated or understood, more would take place. I felt empty and hopeless.

Despite this chaos, the hills behind the granite buildings, covered with dazzling autumn-colored oak, chestnut, alder, and aspen trees, gave me a sense of peace. This was a refuge, a fortress protecting us all from the madness of the outside world. But outside the oasis of the autumn-colored hills, the serenity of the campus was vulnerable. We were all changing—the university system, the lecture rooms, professors, the atmosphere of classes.

I was with Mang Eui-Soon most of the time because we took many of the same courses. He seemed to be always in a state of ultimate happiness. His family lived at Hapdong village near to the Seodaemoon. Because the house was located between the Namdaemun Church and the university, he was able to attend early morning services at the church and then go to school without any inconvenience.

One fall afternoon, we sat together in the woods on piles of dry, brittle leaves. The sky was vivid and clear, and the berries of the wild roses under our feet were brilliant crimson. All was still, and I was peaceful. Mang Eui-Soon lay asleep on a heap of the dried leaves, a deep smile on his face. I was convinced again that God's love imbued him and that he trusted God without reservation.

I thought of his daily routines. At five o'clock he attended the early morning church service and then visited Severance Hospital to help patients, changing their beds or leading worship services. After returning home for breakfast, he hurried to school. When I tried to persuade him to stop his morning hospital visitations, he responded with his peculiar smile.

"This church was built by Dr. Horace N. Allen,[19] an American missionary and medical doctor, for patients and staff from the hospital. The hospital is within the premises of Namdaemun Church; Severance Hospital belongs to the family of Namdaemun Church. The visits to the hospital are the fruit of my early morning prayers. How could I pray only for myself and not do anything for them? I don't do this by myself," he said. "He who is in me does it. I just follow him."

Through the Furnace of Trials

The sense of comfort and security enveloping Mang Eui-Soon's four family members did not last the year. Mang Eui-Soon's mother, who had just turned fifty, died suddenly of a stroke.

---

19. Horace N. Allen was the first American medical doctor missionary who arrived in 1884 and consulted with King Kojong, the second-to-last Korean emperor. Allen founded the first Western hospital and medical school in 1885, in Seoul, now called Severance Hospital, and was the founder of Korea Mission Work.

This was the third death in his family. I could only watch him suffer. He dearly loved his mother, but his grief did not stop there. A few days after his mother's funeral, his remaining sister died after a short illness.

With all the tragedy affecting Mang Eui-Soon, I began to doubt the existence of God, and my faith was unsettled. Where is the God of mercy? Where is God's righteousness in all that is happening? What is wrong with Mang Eui-Soon that God should take what is so precious to him? Why can't God see his loyalty and the purity of his soul?

Then the thought occurred to me that God might not be doing this. Maybe the devil had devised this scheme to shake Mang Eui-Soon's faith and his commitment to God. Perhaps the devil was testing him like Job to see if he really would love God under these circumstances. God had promised his love, but God's power had not prevented the loss of those whom he loved so much. The poison of doubt worked within me.

Mang Eui-Soon's home was a picture of desolation and mourning because of these tragedies happening so quickly together. With the sudden loss of his wife and children, the elder Mang, who had possessed such a strong faith and determination, now looked like someone about to collapse. I spent a night with Mang Eui-Soon at his house in Hapdong. Later that night, he confided to me his feelings about his mother.

"Only the human being possesses the word 'mother,' and it is more than a word; it is the echo of a soul. Even if I lost all ability to speak except for the word 'mother,' the means to communicate, to love, would still be alive."

"When all these things happened to you, I struggled to keep my faith," I told him honestly. "How could this terrible thing happen to such a pious and faithful family? I cannot come to terms with this."

Mang Eui-Soon was silent for a while, almost in a trance. "While going through this grief, I felt as if the sky were collapsing over me. I thought about Job. Sleepless at night, I read the Book of Job. At first it did not console me at all, because I could not identify with him. Job was a legendary character, but I am a living human being. Rather than comforting me, it amplified my grief and pain. I could not pray, either. This scared me.

"Then I saw myself as one who had boasted of offering many things to God. My pride had given me a high score in my eyes. I was shocked as I recognized my attempts to force my own standards onto God, and I thought to myself that God had good reasons to take so many things away from me. I fasted several days and confessed my wrongdoings and the shame and sorrow of human limitations that I could not overcome. Then the Holy Spirit instructed me to open my eyes to the meaning of the sufferings Job had undergone."

I spoke up. "I'm confused. Job was blameless and upright, one who feared God and who turned away from evil. God was proud of him and loved him, but Satan challenged his sincerity."

He responded quietly, "God let Satan do this."

This answer annoyed me, and I raised my voice, "How can you call this love?"

"God wanted to offer Job a victory," Mang Eui-Soon answered. "He wanted him to be a winner. He wanted him to be a son who would not be crushed by evil or suffering. Don't you think that this is genuine love? A victory or defeat from God's perspective is totally different from the world's view. How can we understand God's purpose when he chastens us in order to shape us? We understand it after the suffering. Job confessed: 'I had heard of thee by the hearing of the ear, but now my eye sees thee; therefore I despise myself, and repent in dust and ashes' (Job 42).

"Trials and human suffering are able to break down our egocentric standard. I could not yet view myself through the eyes of the Lord but through my own eyes. I grieved for my mother, sisters, and brother because I did not know the joy they now experience in heaven."

I challenged him by saying, "This kind of suffering will not have a positive impact on non-Christians."

"That is also a human judgment," he responded. When his smile revealed such peace and warmth, I could not believe his grief had ended in such a short time. There was a mystery about him—his unshakable determination to embrace his faith and stand ready for any hardships.

Unrequited Love

Because American missionaries had established the university, students attending the school were encouraged to follow the motto of the university and conform to the Christian code and ethics even though the founding spirit had died out for the most part. The Christian Student Fellowship was one of the oldest organizations on campus. They held their worship meetings around eight o'clock in the morning. Only about ten members attended this morning service regularly. The worship room was unheated, and we warmed our hands by blowing on them. It was a quiet place to visit for meditation or to read the Bible.

I became acquainted with a girl whose name was Kim Young-Joo. The second daughter of a businessman and church elder, she was studying English language and literature. She became a member of the core group of our Christian Student Fellowship. Her vibrant presence enlivened a room. She was intelligent, friendly, and perceptive, and her humor made us laugh. She was spontaneous and exuded confidence as she performed piano solos or accompanied others during Christmas activities in our Christian Student Fellowship.

One morning, coming out of the prayer room, Kim Young-Joo stopped me and asked, "I have noticed that at this time of the week you go to the library. Today, could we talk instead?"

I readily agreed to this, and while we were walking, my heart beat faster as I tried to imagine why she wanted to talk with me. It was too cold to talk outside, so we found an empty lecture room. As soon as Kim Young-Joo sat down, she blurted out something that she had obviously had great difficulty in holding back.

"How is Mang Eui-Soon doing these days?" she asked. Unable to grasp her intention, I was at a loss as to what I could say to this totally unexpected question. "Are you a close friend of Mang Eui-Soon?" she asked. "I imagine that you helped him a lot at the time of his mother's death and more recently at the loss of his sister."

"I don't think I helped him a lot," I answered, "but I have tried to be with him through all of this."

"Why did you not inform me of these things?"

I responded that they were personal and that only a few close friends knew about them.

"Because I am a woman?" she asked.

"No," I exclaimed. "He did not want it."

She raised her voice. "It isn't important whether he wants it or not; we are all family members in Christ."

I apologized to her and said that I hadn't realized she was so concerned. "Mang Eui-Soon is doing well by relying on his Christian faith," I said.

She turned away and spoke in anger. "You said that he was supported by his faith. What is faith? Why do people assign hard things in life to faith? The sorrow in human life is still sorrow, and grief is still grief. I heard that you and Mang Eui-Soon live as close as brothers. Death has left him bereft of his mother and sisters, and he has only his father. Are you going to throw him away to faith? Do you think that a faithful person has no sensitivity? Do you mean that the only way of coping is to become like an iron man?" Kim Young-Joo confronted me acrimoniously while tears welled up in her eyes. I stood there dumbfounded.

"That is not what I mean," I said. "I don't understand him either. He said that the Christian faith enables us to overcome hardships by means of love. He said that God wants us to be winners. I believe that he is pressing toward that goal. It is ludicrous for me to feel sorry for him. I am more miserable than he is! His strength is beyond my comprehension."

Signs of the coming of spring were evident outside the window, and I realized that an entirely new world was opening up to Kim Young-Joo. It wasn't that it was right or wrong, good or bad, happy or sad; but more that an ominous end loomed.

I had thought of her as a naive, innocent female student, and I felt awkward thinking of her with Mang Eui-Soon. Who was I to advise her?

Her deliberate and persistent approach to Mang Eui-Soon surprised me. She was like a lark, fluttering around him. Contrary to my worries, Mang Eui-Soon's response to her was completely natural, spontaneous, and amicable. Kim Young-Joo now regularly attended early morning service at the Namdaemun Church and also accompanied Mang Eui-Soon to Severance Hospital for the visitation service. Of course I never discussed this with him. But I was curious about the mysterious harmony between them.

The sunny spring gave way to summer, and Kim Young-Joo often visited me. We walked along the trails among the trees in the hills behind our campus as if we were intimate friends or lovers. One day she suddenly spoke with great anxiety. "Do you know that Mang Eui-Soon is planning to leave the school?"

"Really?" I asked with astonishment.

"Did he ever talk to you about this? I thought that because you are studying in the same department, you might have discussed his determination to become a minister. This school does not provide much help to students who want to become ministers," she said.

We had once discussed that possibility, and I recalled that Mang Eui-Soon was worried about it. But why tell Kim Young-Joo, instead of me? I was hurt to be hearing this from her and blurted, "Mang Eui- Soon is the type of person who can handle his problems by himself, and once he has made his decision, he sticks with it. I am rather surprised that he has discussed it with you."

Kim Young-Joo understood quickly what I meant. "You think that I have discussions with him? For heaven's sake, no! We talk like strangers, in spite of our long friendship. I suggested to him that he transfer to another department because I think theology is a waste of time. Imagine Mang Eui-Soon studying such a sterile subject as theology! He is too bright and talented for that! Religious Christians insist that all things are meant for the glory of God, but why do they confine themselves to theology or church-related careers? Do they think that is the only way to glorify God? Do they think that it is not possible to contribute to the glory of God by enjoying beauty or nature, the vitality of youth, or the joy of learning and studying? He could work on literature. His writing is very moving and inspirational. Yes, he could be a novelist, a poet. I even asked him to transfer to commerce, political science, or law. Even the arts, like music, would be fine. You are studying music, and I begged him to study music with you."

"Why did you beg him?" I asked.

"I do not want him to graduate in theology."

I asked her for whose benefit she was acting.

"He is bright, and I cannot imagine he would rather become a minister," she answered.

"Then I presume that your intention is to fit Mang Eui-Soon into your own plans," I commented.

She blurted, "I don't know! I don't know!" She threw her face on her hands, pulling up her knees. Because she could not change her plans to fit those of Mang Eui-Soon, she was determined to bring him into line with her own agenda. She hadn't experienced many problems or poverty, having grown up in a wealthy environment. She was disappointed to find that he stood firm in his own plan. "Whatever I say, he accepts me, but he never looks into my world."

I didn't want to listen to her anymore, but she continued. "Why can't it just be a delight? Why does love sometimes mean such deep sorrow? You are one of his closest friends. You know him. What should I do? Even though I need him desperately, I don't really know him at all. Why is that? He is far away from me, in a place that I cannot reach."

What could I tell her about Mang Eui-Soon? Although we spent our boyhood together, and I watched him grow up and remembered his painful past, can I say that I know him? His family, background, character, hobbies, talents, and the sorrow and pain he carries? Do these really sum up what I know about him? When he was young, he seemed to have something unique, a mark that set him apart. I still see the mark at times, but I still don't know what that means. He has a childlike naiveté but also enormous potential energy. Sometimes I think I know all there is to know about him, but other times I feel that I really do not know him at all. We don't have to talk a lot, and I never feel any discomfort when we are quiet, but I often feel as if I had conversed with him on a deep level because of the insights I gain. He has a mystique about him.

He is big and confident, but he has a soft smile unlike anyone else's. While studying for his classes, he is also involved in many other things, but he never appears overburdened. No one notices how hard he is working because he makes himself available to anyone who comes to him for help.

When I think of him, I think about God, too, and I am genuinely thankful, but I also fear these feelings about him. I am afraid that liking him so much, and longing to be like him, might be affecting my perception. As a friend of Mang Eui-Soon, I can't ignore Kim Young-Joo's agony, but how can I help her? How could I solve her problems with Mang Eui-Soon? I concluded that my part was just to listen to her story.

Answering a Call

I often spotted Mang Eui-Soon and Kim Young-Joo together. Sometimes they were walking on the campus, eating lunch together in the woods, or sitting on a hillside at the back of the school of theology building. They appeared to be in love. It looked like Mang Eui-Soon would do what Kim Young-Joo wanted, and they would eventually marry. If he did not intend to accept Kim Young-Joo's plan, why was he so openly close to her?

Then he told me that he was going to Choson Seminary. This was a great shock to me, and I tried to persuade him not to go. He replied, "This university cannot provide me with a diploma qualifying me to be a minister. I love this school, and I had thought that we could spend five years here together."

I could imagine how much agony he had undergone in coming to this decision, and I wanted to cheer him up, but instead I asked him, "Do you really want to be a minister?"

He dropped his head and was quiet. "I don't know yet," he said. "But I have to follow that path."

For a few days before the term examinations, we did not see Kim Young-Joo at school. I was anxious about her. Then Mang Eui-Soon came to me and asked my advice. He said that her father, an elder of a church, had sent a messenger saying that he wanted to see him.

"Why does he want to see you? Do you have any hunches?"

"Her father might have heard Kim Young-Joo's story," Mang Eui-Soon said.

"What did she say?" I asked. "Did you give her some promise?"

Mang Eui-Soon smiled. "Do you believe I was that close to her?" he asked. His attitude made me uneasy. While he went to visit to Kim Young-Joo's father, I had waited nervously for him in his house. When he came back in the late evening, the long summer sun almost set, it was as if he had returned from the battlefield.

"How did it go?" I asked.

"She is sick, so sick she may not be able to write her examinations. She had nagged her father," he said tersely.

"How did she persuade him to call you? How did he treat you?"

"He was friendly, but stern. He asked the same questions that his daughter had asked me," he said. "He wanted me to withdraw my application for studying for the ministry."

"How could an elder of the church ask such a thing?"

"Because he loves his daughter so dearly," he said. "Her father is probably puzzled by me now."

"Did he show any interest in trying to understand you?"

"He feels sorry for his daughter," he said.

"She may even miss the term examination."

Mang Eui-Soon looked so dejected.

Observing his attitude, I asked, "Why does Eros pick a reluctant suitor? There are many young men who are drawn to her. I don't understand either her stubbornness or, in fact, yours. You could persuade her to follow you, to be by your side."

Mang Eui-Soon shook his head. "Do you have any real reason to shun her?"

He gazed at me and said firmly, "I cannot let her hold on to me."

I thought I understood what he was saying. "Yes, she is different from your mother or your sisters. They were delicate, but solid . . . calm and loving. She doesn't have what you want. She's bright, agile, intelligent, and sharp, but not for you!"

"No," he said. "That is not the reason." He stopped me with a painful glance and talked very carefully, as if he were showing hidden artifacts to me. "She is not able to cope with the pain."

"Why not? Is it because she is too spoiled, because she has been brought up in a rich family?"

"No, not necessarily," he answered. "There are two types of people. One that can handle pain and one that cannot, and she is the latter type. I don't want to see her suffer because of me. I really love her; therefore, she is the cause of my anguish, my pain. But it cannot be, ever!"

"You have made a hasty conclusion," I challenged. "Love can be nurtured over a lifetime together."

He answered, "But I don't have time. I don't have the time to spend on it."

This was one of those moments when the mark shone on him. He was looking at me with clear eyes, but protesting against himself. I cruelly grilled him with more questions. "The comment that you made, that you don't have time, seems to be a calculated selfishness, meaning that when you serve God, you think that all other things will distract you."

"No," he said. "I feel that I don't have such time to spend. Not on such things."

Even though he appeared to want me to stop, my questions went on. "She is very sick. Are you going to leave her alone like that?"

"I cannot go to her. That's out of bounds. I really cannot go. There are other people who desperately need my help. She is not the one before whom I should be kneeling down."

I retorted, "Is there a distinction between the love of Christ and of people? Everyone is our neighbor, and whenever they need help, we should help them."

"There is always a priority."

"What if something serious happens to her? Is she really ill? Her father called you for help."

He replied, "Children should know when to stop insisting, when their tactics do not work. Soon she will be fine," he said. "She will come to school for the term exam."

His predictions were correct. Kim Young-Joo came to school and wrote the examinations for all her courses. It was not only Kim Young-Joo who was pale. Mang Eui-Soon was pale and haggard as he wrote his exam. He seemed so tired after the examination that I commented on this during lunch.

"You know that at the new semester you will move to Choson Seminary. Why, then, did you work so hard preparing for this exam? You said that courses taken in this university are not even going to be taken into account. You look gaunt. Take a rest."

"It is not because of the exam," he said.

Then I thought of Kim Young-Joo. Mang Eui-Soon was caught in a peculiar predicament: he could not continue to see her as if nothing had happened between them, nor could he stop seeing her, nor treat her like a stranger, as if something serious had happened between them.

He was in agony. "Is the most difficult time over?" I asked.

He shook his head. "Nothing is more difficult for a person than fighting against himself." He dropped his head dismally, as if he were confessing his own sins. I could see that he was in agonizing turmoil: between his logic that he could not accept Kim Young-Joo, while at the same time finding that he could not liberate himself completely from a desire for her. I could not say anything. In the face of his soulful anguish, my friendship was no help to him.

When the exams were nearly over, the city of Seoul began to undergo more turmoil. The chairman of the People's Labor Party, Yeo Un-Hyong[20], was assassinated. The nineteen-year-old assassin, proud of his act, said during interrogation, "Regardless of the right or left, anyone who disturbs the political situation of the country for the sake of our unifica-

20. See footnote 18.

tion should be eliminated, that scum wiped out. I am not a murderer. I am a righteous man."

Mang Eui-Soon and I sat facing each other, lamenting the situation. He was seriously worried. "This is just the beginning. Where is this country heading?"

His remarks made me afraid for our country. He went on. "The leaders of this country devoted their entire lives to our independence. Having returned to their liberated country, why do they live in hostility against each other? Why can't they accept each other? Why should they be slaughtered in this land for which they devoted their whole lives? Oh, I cannot understand all this!

"Man is like a flower in the field," he continued. "'For the sun rises with its scorching heat and withers the grass; its flower falls, and its beauty perishes' (James 1). While our lives may blossom, in the end they will fade away. What we should seek is something that will not wither."

The skepticism crouching deep in my heart erupted. "It is impossible to find!"

"The answer does not come from this world. The process is more important than the result."

I challenged him then. "But you have a goal, a clear one, not of this world. But I don't have the willpower to let go of this material reality."

He went on speaking, with warmth, "What is there for us in the world? It is not a matter of either holding on or letting go of this world. When we are obsessed with how to get something out of this world, we fall into a trap. This world is a stepping-stone to eternity and a shadow of what is to come. We are afraid to let go of this world because we believe there is something, an offering of pleasure, in this world. It is eternity we are pursuing. There is nothing worth attaching ourselves to or even hating in this world."

I sharply retorted, "What about this country, our native land? If we had a country free of troubles, we wouldn't have to suffer such miseries."

"It is our destiny, and we should face it. It is important that we embrace any conditions or circumstances. We are meant to find the meaning rather than whine about why we have to suffer," he chuckled.

That autumn, Mang Eui-Soon took the entrance examination for Choson Seminary and enrolled in the preparatory course. He moved, and we rarely saw each other, but whenever we did meet, we were always comfortable with each other.

Choson Seminary was near the Dongja-Dong neighborhood. After visiting his school, I was disappointed with the size of the campus and the facilities. He noticed my reaction and grinned in explanation. "I am very happy to live close to school. Since the church and Severance Hospital and school are so close, I can walk back and forth from school to church. As you know, Ms. La Chang-Seok is nearby. Whenever I miss my mother, I can visit her. I am just thankful."

Despite his hectic schedule, he carried out his responsibilities faithfully. It was difficult for him to allocate time other than for school and church, but he could usually make himself available to me.

He took charge of the class of the middle school in the church and almost lived with them. The class grew immensely under his leadership. It started with ten students, soon grew to a hundred, and eventually reached 150 students. They worked hard together in Bible class, choir, and mission service.

We met often to prepare the winter program, and Kim Young-Joo also worked with us. She wanted to participate in any activities organized by Mang Eui-Soon, even after he moved. As her summer fever had clearly healed, Kim Young-Joo once again was lively and witty. She behaved naturally with Mang Eui-Soon and seemed not to recall the summer incident of his rejection of her. His attitude toward her was consistent. He was kind to her without closeness.

It was December, and the weather was unusually mild as if preparing to snow, but things were still very heated on the treacherous political scene. A general election in Korea was proposed by the United Nations, and the motion was passed after hot debate. The Korea Committee, consisting of eight countries—France, Canada, Australia, India, the Philippines, El Salvador, China, and Ceylon—began its work. Meanwhile, another leader, Chang Deuk-Soo, a political director of the Korea Democratic Party, was shot to death. The winter forest around the university now had a lonely and silent beauty. The barren branches had lost their leaves and were surrounded by gray winter clouds. It was extremely gloomy and lonely, except for the birds flying over the trees.

It was at that time that Kim Young-Joo visited me. We walked together to Namdaemun Church, where I had agreed to assist her with the choir and a drama for the middle-school students. Kim Young-Joo walked ahead as if she had forgotten someone was beside her. I followed silently behind her. Suddenly she stopped and stared at me and said, “I don’t understand him. But I love him. You thought that I had given up, didn’t you? But I cannot give him up.”

Her eyes were burning, and I could not look at her. “Anytime and anywhere he is always with me, in my thoughts. But I realize that he will never be mine. The closer he is to me, the clearer it becomes that he is in his own world.”

When I asked if she would be able to change her attitude toward him, she replied, “I want to show him a more profound meaning of life. I believe that his awkward way to faith is not all there is to life. It is so eccentric. He can sacrifice and devote his life to other miserable and unhappy people, so why does he ignore my misery? Isn’t that hypocrisy, the worst kind of hypocrisy?”

“I’m sorry. I don’t understand him either, but he loves you dearly,” I replied.

“Can he only follow the will of God by becoming a minister? I don’t think so. I think such stubborn and persistent faith comes from a sick kind of heroism,” she said.

“No!” I retorted. “That isn’t his motivation. He is trying to do his best to remain faithful to God.”

She blurted, “I am annoyed that he wastes his talents for music, literature, and other things.”

"God never loses. It is God who gave him talent. God will use his talent to the fullest, and God will give him even more to use."

Kim Young-Joo dug into the fallen leaves with her foot. "He is such a slave to that middle-school class. I visited the middle-school class of K Church, which claims to be comparable to his class. The atmosphere was quite different. The kids were very refined and vibrant. After finishing the program, they could become very competitive and successful. But the kids under his direction are lamentably fragile and feeble. Young people should demonstrate passion and strength. Sometimes he takes them to the overnight prayer meeting. He is like a man always racing towards misery."

Kim Young-Joo seemed frozen. I felt her pain, but who can heal the pain of love? Heavy hearted, I wanted to help her in whatever way I could. I spoke honestly to her. "I don't think any human will be able to make him change his mind."

"Then who can?" she asked.

"Only God can," I said. "When we suffer, we think it will never end. But this will end. In time, you and I will have a good friend, a minister. Then we can help him with our special friendship."

Kim Young-Joo laughed ironically with a look that matched the gloomy winter sky. "He has inflicted so much pain on me. Now he wants to be a holy minister?"

She said this as a joke, but I was as shocked by the words as if stabbed by a knife.

Tempestuous Night

Despite the bloodshed and social upheaval, the change of seasons proceeded unhindered. The poet Lee Sang-Hwa asked, "Will spring return to a captured land?" We wondered how we dare sing about the return of spring when the land lay pillaged and divided. What kind of spring would it be?

On February 28, 1948, the Korea Committee of the United Nations passed a resolution by a vote of thirty-one to two to hold a general election on May 10. The plan was to establish a separate government of South Koreans. But Kim Ku and Kim Kyu-Shik insisted that the division of the country should be blocked at any cost. They proposed talks between South and North Korea and were optimistic about persuading Kim Il-Sung in North Korea by appealing to his Korean patriotism.

Meanwhile, a riot broke out on Cheju Island, which was isolated from the mainland. Early on the morning of April 3, 1948, after well-organized planning, the rioters attacked a storage room, stealing ammunition and weapons. They captured other armories, attacked police stations in Cheju City, damaged government offices, set fires, and killed people. Springtime in Cheju Island was shoved aside ruthlessly. The island became an altar of blood afloat in the ocean.

The storm of rioting was not easily subdued. The population of this formerly quiet island had been only 150,000, but after the liberation from the Japanese, thousands of Koreans taken captive who had served the Japanese army or the Chinese Eighth Route Army were returned to this island, almost doubling the population. The island provided a refuge for those who were engaged in criminal activities or who wanted to avoid prosecution.

At that time, the South Korea Labor Party, which had created chaos in Seoul right after the liberation, infiltrated Cheju Island. They harshly criticized the government, and the islanders were persuaded to join with the party to wage a full-scale antigovernment uprising. They had plenty of weapons and ammunition, which had been recovered from the defeated Japanese or captured at police stations. Furthermore, the dense forest and the gorges provided a natural fortress. Antimissile caverns made by the Japanese army, which could accommodate more than 200,000 people, provided an advantage for their guerrilla warfare. Many of the government officials were sympathetic to the guerrillas, and this gave them another advantage over the regular army forces.

The guerrillas rampaged and killed more than a hundred policemen and members of their families. They also killed government officials and civilians. Every night, they attacked and plundered civilians.

Even though this occurred on an isolated island, it could not be overlooked. The army was not able to quell the rebellion quickly. The bloodshed continued. Our country had faced many invaders and had suffered many disasters, but somehow we had come through them all. Why were we suddenly willing to attack, shoot, and destroy one another, just as we had became free from the poisonous teeth of an occupying power? This rebellion was localized, but no one knew how it might eventually develop.

Kim Ku and Kim Kyu-Shik returned home from their trip to North Korea, both of them having been manipulated by Kim

Il-Sung. His plan was to establish his People's Republic over all Korea. The delegates announced that they had received three promises from the North. First, they would continue to deliver electricity to the South; second, they would open the Yeonbaek water reservoir; and third, they would allow the return of Mr. Cho Man-Shik to the South. However, no one believed them, not even the children.

The newly liberated country was extremely poor. People, hungry and in rags, roamed the countryside for food but found nothing to fill their stomachs. Electricity was only available for short periods at night; candles were so scarce that kerosene lamps were usually used.

What made us most miserable was not hunger or poverty but the lack of faith and trust in the future of our country and our people. We were perplexed because there was no clear reason for a division among our people. We wanted to do something to make it better, to repair what had been torn apart. We often gathered for prayer meetings and to help farmers, for this was their busiest season of the year. We worked on gospel outreach and medical service as much as we could.

One day in May I had arrived early for an appointment and was shocked to see Kim Young-Joo entering the room, her face flushed with anger. She walked straight toward me, and I stood up awkwardly because I could not figure out what was wrong.

"Would you please come outside with me for a moment?" she said, her eyes piercing.

"Why?" I asked. "It's almost time for my appointment."

"It will only take few minutes," she insisted. Being uncomfortable with Kim Young-Joo's anger and embarrassed by her behavior, I looked around the room. She apologized but repeated her request.

I asked her again what was going on, and again she responded with anger. "You'll see when we get there. Then you'll understand. You may even feel sorry for me. I'm not angry. I feel a great sadness."

Regardless of what she said, she was angry. I kept quiet and followed her. She walked across the Insa-Dong neighborhood intersection to the tram tracks and entered Pagoda Park. She moved quickly, as if someone were waiting for her. I almost had to run to keep up with her. There were people gathered under the shade of the few trees, and I heard the beat of a drum.

Then I saw Mang Eui-Soon, beating a drum hanging around his neck and crying out, "Repent! Heaven is at hand. Believe in the Lord Jesus Christ. Then you and your household will be saved!"

The many students gathered around him began to sing hymns loudly as they handed out leaflets. I was stunned as I watched them. After the singing, Mang Eui-Soon started shouting again, "Repent! Brothers and sisters, repent! Remember the destruction of Sodom and Gomorrah. God blessed us and gave us freedom, but we were neither humble nor thankful. We are still killing each other, shedding blood and plotting destruction. Jesus said, 'If you do not turn from your sins, you will all die like those who were killed when the tower fell on them.' Repent!"

His voice was clear and firm, calling out with an underlying strength to those on that dusty street. He was drenched in sweat from his exertions, and many people on the street ignored him. Others laughed at him, seeing him as little more than a wild man.

Kim Young-Joo looked at me with a strange coldness in her stare. In tears, she asked, "Did you see him? Why does he do that? Why is he ignoring reality and humiliating himself in this way?"

I stared back at her. "This is the freedom he has found. It's wonderful and beautiful, and no one can dare to imitate it. Let him go his way. This is the way he has chosen." I looked away from Kim Young-Joo to watch Mang Eui-Soon beating his drum.

Kim Young-Joo turned her back and walked quietly away. I wasn't sure if she was heading back to our meeting place or somewhere else, but I could not follow her, because Mang Eui-Soon's voice beat in my heart louder than any drum.

The street outreach being carried on by the students of Namdaemun Church became the subject of gossip. Mang Eui-Soon's drum reverberated everywhere. He visited the Seoul railway station, which was a gathering point for people who had fled to the South from North Korea. The gaunt luggage carriers, people sitting dejectedly on their few possessions, people who were anxious and dislocated—all heard Mang Eui-Soon's drumbeat and the message he proclaimed: "Are we seeking only visible things? All that we see or feel is temporary. What we should seek is not what we see with our eyes. Believe that Jesus is with us, even though we cannot see him or touch him. His kingdom is not transient, but invisible. Believe in what is eternal. We can enter his eternal kingdom by trusting the Spirit of Jesus, by trusting his eyes and his hands."

People who were cold and hungry got angry v "Crazy *******!" someone shouted at him. "Does Jes you? You have three meals a day, but if your stomach was empty, would you still cry out for Jesus?"

After hearing these charges, Mang Eui-Soon began to fast before he went out to preach on the street. He asked his students not to drink or smoke. He stressed that we could not overcome poverty unless we first tighten our own belts.

Mang Eui-Soon's street missions continued, even though some people disapproved. There were those who said he was doing too much. Some of the more "intellectual" members of his congregation expressed concern about his outreach methods. They felt his approach to evangelism was outdated and inefficient—too old-fashioned for the times. Others were perplexed that a man of his education would go out into the streets, beating a drum and calling on people to repent and believe in Jesus. One complained, "If people were interested in Jesus, Mang Eui-Soon would scare them away!"

Parents criticized him for gathering his students around him. "They are together day and night," one said. "After morning devotions, they visit the Severance Hospital to care for the patients, and then right after school, they go back to the church for Bible study and choir practice. The cycle never ends. They spend every Friday night in prayer." Despite the complaints of some parents, the enrollment of students at Namdaemun Church grew to over three hundred.

People wondered from where he drew his power. They knew he was a seminary student, and they also knew of his personal tragedy in the abrupt and untimely loss of four family members. They saw how he reached out for Jesus. However, some were offended by his seeming claim to greater faith and spiritual superiority.

There was a clear change in Kim Young-Joo's attitude after the incident at Pagoda Park, however. Now there was a chill between us whenever we met. I did not have another chance to talk to her because she intentionally avoided me. My relationship with her was strained.

Questions kept nagging at me. Why was what Mang Eui-Soon was doing such a shock to her? She, a confessed Christian and her father an elder in the church, had boasted about the lineage of Christians in her family. Why, then, did she treat Mang Eui-Soon like a criminal? Considering her attitude, how could she say that she loved him? She had claimed that she could not give him up. What does she love about him? Does she understand him, even though she professes to cherish him?

Despite the criticism spreading around Mang Eui-Soon, he continued on in the same way. He was like a living tree, thanking the sun when it rises and being grateful for water when it rains.

Whenever I was with him, or thinking about him, I was reminded of a quotation from the writings of Thomas à Kempis: "Strive to withdraw your heart from the love of things, and direct your affections to things invisible." I believe that Mang Eui-Soon saw clearly what others could not, and he moved toward that goal with a single-mindedness, undivided by distractions. I was annoyed that I could not yet see as he saw.

My friend Mang Eui-Soon held the same viewpoint as Thomas à Kempis. They experienced a union with God that transcended time and space.

> Truly, we have eyes and see not. For what concern to us are such things as genera and species? Those to whom the Eternal Word speaks are delivered from uncertainty. From one Word proceed all things . . . Without Him, no one can understand or judge aright. But the man to whom all things are one, who refers everything to One, and who sees everything as in One, that man is enabled to remain steadfast in heart, and can abide at peace with God.[21]

I could not understand why I could not share their view. I knew that I didn't belong, but I didn't know why. What was I seeking? What is eternity? Why do people constantly long for eternity, even though they do not comprehend it? Why are we afraid? Finally, I came to the conclusion that eternity could not be proved with our limited perception, and yet eternity exists in our awareness. The essence of humanity is eternal, and that is the reason why we ceaselessly aspire to it. We were cut off from eternity; and now, through our suffering in this flawed and chaotic world, we yearn for our original essence.

Mang Eui-Soon and Thomas à Kempis were in alignment with eternity and with someone who could lead them to it. They gave witness that this someone was Jesus. I could say that I believed in Jesus, but I could not say that I was one with Jesus. This was a great anguish for me.

What is faith all about? I think I believe, but what do I believe? I did not quite understand. How could I be like them?

---

21. Written by Thomas à Kempis, translated and with an introduction by Leo Sherley-Price. Penguin Books, 1952, p. 30. Used by permission.

I should be like them, shouldn't I? It was very confusing. I was afraid and felt as if I were crazy.

I spent the summer traveling, thinking that this would be a way to escape these thoughts. I avoided the Christian Student Fellowship activities and volunteer work with farmers, including mission work, medical service, and summer Bible school. I sent Mang Eui-Soon a few post cards, informing him of my location, but not writing about anything serious. I wandered the country restlessly.

Three years after liberation, chaos, bloodshed, and murder buffeted our country. The political situation was extremely unstable. On May 10, 1948,[22] a general election was held in South Korea. A constitutional assembly was convened on May 31, and on July 2, the National Assembly passed the constitutional organization. On July 17, the National Assembly proclaimed a constitution and named the country the Republic of Korea, and on July 24, Rhee Syngman was elected president with Lee See-Young as vice president. On August 15, three years after Korea's liberation, the government of the Republic of Korea was established, and the new republic was officially inaugurated.

Street Preaching

The pace of school life settled into routine as the fall semester began. Trees started to turn from green to the colors of autumn. Thoughts and work that had been set aside during the

---

22. South Korea held its own general election under UN supervision, and on August 15, 1948, the Republic of Korea was established.

summer were now taken up again. One day, Mang Eui-Soon made an unexpected visit to school to meet me. He said that he had missed the autumn forest.

It had been a long time since we had been in the forest together. In the beauty of the natural surroundings we took time to consider not only the turn of the seasons, but also our own lives.

"Are you still preaching in the streets?" I asked. "Don't you have other things to do? Your studies? Why must you do this kind of preaching?"

"Because when I do, I feel my heart burning inside me. It is not I, but someone within me expressing love. Can you not see it?"

I told him that Kim Young-Joo had totally changed her mind about him after she had watched him in the street from a distance. His shoulders dropped. Looking down at the ground like a child who was being scolded, he scuffed his feet in the dry grass. At that moment, I saw the struggle in his face, a loneliness coming from his conviction that he must hold on to the truth as he saw it, even if others did not understand. He slowly lifted his face and looked at me.

"Are you convinced that what I do is so bad?" he asked.

"It's not a matter of good or bad," I responded. "But this doesn't need to be the only method you choose for outreach."

"Whose opinion is that? Yours or someone else's?"

I was quite at a loss and extremely embarrassed by the sudden exposure of my cowardice. At first, when Kim Young-Joo had taken me to see him preaching at Pagoda Park, I had been moved by his attitude. But then I heard other people belittle his style of outreach as something outdated, a mistake, and I joined them. Angry at my weakness and myself, I answered him, "Why are you asking that? It's your strange way of doing things that I don't like."

Mang Eui-Soon responded tersely, "It may look bad, but I don't have a choice. It is urgent. Time is short."

"Why are you the only one in a hurry? Everyone else seems to be all right."

He buried his face in his hands. "I only know that there is a great urgency. I cannot resist the call to preach." He took a Bible out of his briefcase, opened it to Jeremiah 25, placed it in front of me, and read, "Thus the LORD, the God of Israel, said to me: 'Take from my hand this cup of the wine of wrath, and make all the nations to whom I send you drink it.'"

After reading these verses, he said, "This is about Judah. It's the history of Judah, conquered by Babylon. God controls the history of the world. The things that are happening in this country are inviting the cup of the wine of wrath. As I prayed, God showed me the entire land devastated. I saw corpses strewn on the ground. I cannot erase this vision."

I was at a loss as he described all this to me. "Is there something we can do? Can the youth of this country set an example of righteousness? Can we do something to bring happiness to the people as we struggle for social justice?"

"Did you say 'justice'?" He took his hands away from his face as he spoke again in anguish. "So many people are shouting about justice. They are killing each other with swords in the name of justice."

With certain reluctance, I asked, "Then what preparation do we need?"

"Love."

I was so disappointed at his reply that I laughed. "Love?" I could agree with him that everyone claimed to love, but he maintained that love belongs to God and that we should love through Jesus, the body and soul of love. I asked, "If love belongs to God, doesn't justice also?"

"Yes, God owns everything. But I strongly feel that justice must be sublimated into love. If justice exists as mere justice, that will bring on more fighting, because each person will pull it to his own advantage. Love transcends justice and embraces both, fusing them into a powerful and complete form. Enforcing justice without love will surely result in hurting others as well as ourselves in the end. The ultimate choice offered to the human being is either to find his or her place of humility and kneel down before the Lord, or to reject him. Where people are able to kneel down together, a fountain of living water wells up, and they can all drink together."

The thought of bending my knees made my legs numb, and I stood up right away. Disappointed in myself, I turned on Mang Eui-Soon. "Are you going to continue this preaching?" I asked him for a second time.

"That is not what I am doing," he said.

"What do you mean you are not doing it?"

"Someone in me is doing it."

I stared at him in surprise. He must have entered some kind of madness. His unbearable grief after the loss of his loving family members must have caused him to lose his mind.

On October 29, a Communist insurgency took place in the cities of Yeosu and Sunchon. President Rhee Syngman had gone to Tokyo at the invitation of General Douglas MacArthur. The rebel army spread a false rumor that the president had fled to Japan. Riots coincided with the anniversary of the Russian Revolution, and about three thousand US soldiers from the Fourteenth Regiment stationed in Yeosu City were ordered to move. Suddenly, the rebels fired on the soldiers indiscriminately. Some forty members of the pro-Communist Namro (the South Labor) Party, led by Kim Chee-Hee, had been clandestinely working within the army. The destruction by the rebels did not end there.

On November 2, with the rebels in Yeosu and Sunchon still active, a riot broke out in the Sixth Regiment stationed in Daegu. Members of the Namro Party killed some South Korean army officials in their barracks and then attacked major government offices. The rebel soldiers were estimated at only about four or five hundred in number, with a few civilians among them, but they were able to wreak havoc and devastation upon Daegu City.

Our liberated fatherland continued to suffer the crisis of a divided self. Before one incident could be resolved, trouble broke out elsewhere. People fought against their own people; brother fought against brother. They continued to stab, injure, and kill each other. How do people become like that? When will the bloodshed stop? August 15, 1945, was meant to mark our liberation with our people released from the chains of slavery. We should have helped and comforted each other. Instead we fought with one another.

Missing His Mother

When winter came, we hoped Christmas would be a season of some joy for our gloomy hearts. One night I came to Namdaemun Church to see Mang Eui-Soon. I expected him to be there with the students preparing the Christmas program.

From a dimly lit middle-school classroom came the sound of a tenor voice singing "Ave Maria." Electricity was restricted then, so the overhead light was not on, but a kerosene lamp softly illuminated the room. I stood beside the window, closed my eyes, and listened. It was not music, but a prayer begging the world to stop the rampage. It was a voice calling the world to stop its ruthless greed, competition, and hatred. When the song was over, the room was silent.

I opened the door; he was alone. The kerosene lamp flickered as he sat beside the closed piano, crying. From the evidence of cleaning tools, he must have cleaned the room after sending out his students. Stooped over, crying, he hadn't noticed me. In that moment, the weight of the world pressed heavily on both of us.

He sat up straight when he noticed my approach, his face soaked with tears. "I miss my mother so much," he said quietly. Tears rolled down his face, but he did not wipe them away.

In June 1949, there was a riot in the same parliament in which we had proclaimed our independence. About ten young members of parliament were found to be under the direct influence of the Namro Party, and they had agreed to help pass a bill to order the withdrawal of foreign soldiers. With sixty-two names supporting their petition, they were about to send it to the Korea Committee of the United Nations. But the situation did not turn in their favor. For an independent country to have a foreign army stationed within its borders is not an honorable thing. But in light of the international and national situation, it was appropriate. This was no time to urge withdrawal of these troops from South Korea. All of this showed how blatantly the Communists worked to disrupt South Korea.

As the Communists had penetrated the South Korean parliament, it was almost impossible for civilians to expect security. While the Namro Party was causing unrest in the parliament, the country lost another bright star. National leader Kim Ku was shot to death on June 26, 1949. He had sought national independence without relying on outside help. He had entreated us to bravely follow our own path, to push aside the interference of other countries. He had wanted us to be united and had given his life for his country and his people.

Seoul was frozen by fear and sadness, even in the heat of summer. Everyone was in shock, crying and wailing. On July 5, 1949, the country observed a national funeral ceremony. Everyone wore black mourning bands. There were torrents of tears, and this martyred man was eulogized with genuine grief.

Kwonsa La Chang-Seok

Early in the new year, I received a letter from Mang Eui-Soon.

January 1950

My Dear Friend,

Though it isn't necessary to say, it still is true that one year goes and another comes, but this new year will be special. I have been kneeling in prayer, and midnight has just passed. I am thinking of you as I write.

New Year! We begin with a new day as the sun rises. Or rather, we rise to embrace the new day. I am afraid. I don't know what lies ahead for us in this year 1950.

What will it bring to me and to our people? I feel weight beyond measure on us. The fear that consumes me is clouding my faith. There are times when I feel like a person without any faith at all, and I am so ashamed. For believers, the future is something beyond this world, and it has nothing to do with our present time and space. But I cannot help but think about things that we will eventually face. Sometimes I dream wonderful dreams about this world, building my future and achieving my own goals.

Entering the sixth year of Korean independence, how are we nurturing our young country? It is like a cloth ripped, stitched, and torn at the hands of others. We are biting and slashing each other. What will the year 1950 bring?

Again I pray for this new year, that it would confirm our vitality and that we would see our lives in new perspective. I wish you a happy, meaningful, and beautiful year.

Love,
Mang Eui-Soon

Mang Eui-Soon had a new stepmother, Kwonsa La Chang-Seok. She had been working in the Youngnak Boin Nursing Home and Orphanage operated by Youngnak Presbyterian Church and was a devoted Christian in her fifties who had never married. She radiated elegance and demonstrated warmth and determination in her work with the elderly and orphans.

What surprised us was that she had changed her mind about marriage and had consented to become the wife of Elder Mang. She had worked as the superintendent of Pyongyang Women's Seminary (formerly Pyongyang Women's Bible School) and then with Reverend Han Kyung-Jik as a pastor for eight years at Second Shineuijoo Church and later at an orphanage run by the church, where she supervised the kindergarten teachers. At the time of Korean independence, she became director of a nursing home also run by her church, as well as the director of the orphanage.

There was severe famine at this time, and Miss La's orphans had only tree bark to eat. She had come to South Korea to seek food, intending to stay for a week, but the road was blocked when she attempted to return. Miss La then started to work in Youngnak Boin Nursing Home and Orphanage, but she planned that when the road opened she would go back to the North and the hundred or so orphans and elderly persons who were waiting for her at Namshineuijoo Orphanage.

Apparently it was Mang Eui-Soon who eventually convinced Miss La to marry Elder Mang. I knew her well, having met her when I visited Youngnak Boin with Mang Eui-Soon. She always treated us with warmth and special kindness every time we visited. She was gentle and affectionate but firm and resolute and always devoted to her work. Now that he had a woman to call "Mother," he became livelier and happier. He was very proud of her.

One day in early spring, we had dinner together at my house. He joyfully confided in me that he had waited to see what the year 1950 would bring to him, and it had given him a mother who was prudent, meticulous, and wonderful. He believed that the year would be a happy one.

"Why are you so excited? She has been a mother for many people, for orphans, kindergarten teachers, and even people with senile dementia. Now you have a monopoly on her. You should apologize!" I teased. "Now I would like you to sing while I accompany you on the piano," I said. "And I want you to sing until I let you stop."

He sang through his repertoire of songs from Beethoven, Schubert, and Mendelssohn. He sang all the songs with such zeal that he forgot I was there. How exquisite is the sound that comes from the human vocal cords, both soft and powerful. Now I knew why Kim Young-Joo loved him so much. So much that she stamped the floor in frustration about him. When I heard his singing, the crazy world stopped its spinning and became silent, listening. He sang, not caring what others felt about his singing.

"Tell me more about your parents. How are they? Does your father still call your stepmother 'Madame Kwonsa,' even though they are sharing the same bedroom?"

"I guess so, but he cannot help it," he replied. "My father promised her before they were married that he would call her Madame Kwonsa. He not only calls her by her title, but he pays the utmost respect to her."

"That seems a bit unusual," I said.

"Not really. They like things this way. It makes them feel comfortable. They suit each other. My stepmother is a wonderful woman. Isn't she still beautiful? And she cares for our family so well. Taking all this into account, I wonder why she had not thought of marriage before. I believe that she is an angel who has come to restore our devastated home."

"God must have felt sorry for a son and a father left alone in this world."

"I guess so," he said, smiling. "I'm going to the army hospital in Bupyung tomorrow. As God gave my new mother to me, I interpret it as a reason to double my workload."

"The army hospital in Bupyung? That's a surprise."

"A nurse army captain working at that hospital asked our minister to send a pastor. He could not find a suitable pastor, so he asked me to go."

I stood there in the dark as he walked away. While watching his receding silhouette, I felt a strange desolation, like a cold wind sweeping my heart. He was happy now. He had a new mother, he was studying what he wanted to study, he was finding meaning in his church ministry, and he was doing new things. He was not a lonely man now, nor carrying an undue burden of sorrow. But I sensed a tragedy hovering over him. I tried to dispel this notion, but I could not shake off these feelings.

A Budding Relationship with Captain Yu

After the spring semester began, Kim Young-Joo attended a morning worship service, breaking her long hibernation. As the bell chimed to end the first class, the boisterous students moved out. The air was filled with a spring haze, and buildings and people seemed to be bursting with energy. Smiling as she approached, she said that she had come to see me. "We've known each other for a long time, but you don't really know me," she said. "Why don't we take a walk together on this beautiful day?"

I could not refuse her. We went outside. She was smiling. I had heard rumors of her dating other young men, and I knew that she had not recently been attending early morning devotions nor participating in volunteer hospital work. I was curious about her relationship with Mang Eui-Soon, but I also thought that it would be better for them to go their separate ways.

She talked about the lovely spring weather as we walked along the trail. I didn't respond because I realized that she was avoiding the real subject. "Nature is so mysterious and exquisite," she said. "It calms the mind, as we appreciate its beauty and charm. But humans are quite different. Mang Eui-Soon is different. I cannot understand him."

I kept silent and continued to walk beside her. This response was what I had feared. I was embarrassed to hear that she was still struggling with this problem. With a deep sigh she asked if I knew about his recent situation, that he had been going to the army hospital to conduct the Sunday services.

"Yes," I said. "I heard about this from him."

"But you do not know that he has been having fun with a young girl while working there," she said with a short laugh.

I was at a loss to say anything. Finally I asked, "What do you mean 'having fun' while working there?"

"He works for God and has dates with a girl." She was laughing, but it was not sincere laughter. It covered an unbearable pain and anger that lingered on her face like a shadow. "I have seen them."

"With your own eyes?" I asked.

"Several times I have seen them walking together."

"Just seeing them walking together is no proof that they are in love," I protested.

Kim Young-Joo continued her story. "When I saw them the first few times, I thought that they might just be friends. But last weekend when I saw them coming out of the cinema, I could see that they were definitely a couple. The movie has explicit erotic content. They are in a relationship, even if they try to hide it."

"Whoever he is going with, I'm sure that she is safe," I said.

"The woman is seven years older than he is," Kim Young-Joo continued. Her face was pale and she spoke with a chill in her voice.

"She is a nurse, an army captain, working in the army hospital in Bupyung," I said. "A beautiful woman. From the fact that he hasn't introduced you, you have deduced that she is very dear to him." I laughed.

"Why are you laughing? Is it silly? She is older than him by seven years and could be an expert in anything. She will do more for him than I will."

"Kim Young-Joo," I said, "your hasty conclusion is making you miserable. Why are you letting this happen?"

"I don't know. I don't understand what attracts me to him, but I cannot give him up. I thought that my feelings had been buried, but they have resurfaced."

The bright sun contrasted with her wretchedness. She shook her head as if making an important decision. "I will not give up. Wherever he goes, and whoever he associates with, is not my business, but it is impossible for me to let him go."

I did not visit Mang Eui-Soon specifically to discuss Kim Young-Joo, but when I saw him next, I could not hold back. "Who is the young woman who accompanied you to the cinema?" I asked, feeling remorseful about asking, but watching for his reaction.

"The lady is Miss Yu. She is a nurse army captain from the army hospital. We went to a movie together," came his answers, without hesitation. His calmness made my question seem crass. "It is true that I was with her," he said, "but I don't know why this would upset people." He was smiling as he said this, in contrast to Kim Young-Joo's behavior.

"I like to spend time with her. Miss Yu is very comfortable to be with. If some people think she is my girlfriend, they are wrong. She is not that kind of person."

I reminded him that she was an older woman. "Yes, I guess so," he said. "Why are people even discussing this? She is different."

"Human nature is not as simple as you think," I responded.

"If you don't trust my judgment, you can see for yourself. You will notice this right away."

Our conversation was candid, and his response was so natural, that my questions and doubts put me to shame. Changing my attitude, I said, "Then I would be delighted to meet her." He promised to introduce us on the coming Sunday.

The May sunlight, blazing as we traveled by train to the city of Inchon, made everything we saw from the train windows like a colorful dance. Behind the army hospital were low rising hills. Even though old and gloomy, the hospital came alive in the bright sunshine, but inside, the army hospital was dark. The dimly lit corridors emitted a pungent stench coming from the seriously wounded patients. The smell of antiseptic almost overwhelmed me. I was shocked as we walked through the main hall and entered the ward. Then I heard a woman's voice. "Welcome, I was expecting you."

My friend stood beside me to greet her, but all I could do was stand still and stare at her. She was like the stem of a magnolia tree. She wore a uniform, but more than that, her beauty, poise, and elegance no uniform could cover up. More than her physical appearance surprised me, for she carried a weight of sorrow, although "sorrow" does not seem an adequate word to describe it. It was something bigger than that. She did not seem to notice my apprehension and approached us happily.

"You are a friend of Mr. Mang Eui-Soon, aren't you? We welcome you." She was spontaneous and friendly as if we had met before. "We still have some time before the worship service, time for a tea break. I'll be right back after finishing my work."

Graciously she showed us to her room. In the well-lit room, I looked closely at her. She was elegant and beautiful. Why had I had some premonition when I first saw her?

I had not given much thought as to how serious the condition of some of the patients would be, despite the strong odor. On entering the corridor, I saw a pale young man lying on his bed and staring at us with big eyes, totally paralyzed. In another bed, a middle-aged man was paralyzed in the lower part of his body.

Captain Yu and my friend Mang Eui-Soon sat beside these men, holding their hands and praying for them. They sang hymns while they massaged their bodies. Mang Eui-Soon cared for the middle-aged man, while Captain Yu massaged the younger one. The younger patient, stricken by grief, despair, and fear, showed no emotion. The older man was full of anger. He had no peace in his eyes, only rage and bitterness. They helped the patients change position every five or ten minutes. While singing hymns and offering physical care, their actions seemed natural and well matched.

Then Mang Eui-Soon moved silently to the chapel for the worship service. There were about two hundred mobile patients who were singing while waiting for the service to start. While he gave a message from the pulpit, he seemed like someone new to me. There was an aura about him. After the worship service, he returned to the room where the serious patients were. He again gave them massages while singing hymns. He ate dinner with the patients, and then he left.

On the train ride home, he said, "For me, this hospital is a symbol of the pain and fear that is all around us. I am angry about human wickedness and despair when I see these patients who are totally paralyzed and cannot even die by their own will. They were young and full of vigor, and suddenly, bullets devastated their lives. Is war worth it? In olden times, fights were between tribes who fought because of their differences. These young men were told that they were brave to fight for their country. What has the country gained from their sacrifice? Are things any different or any better? In the face of their misery, there is nothing to be said. I feel sorrow and shame."

Mang Eui-Soon gazed at the sunset. Tears rolled down his cheeks. "Societal and structural evils are eroding our country, and individuals are powerless. Each person in those hospital beds has given his whole life to the cause of war. But the government counts them and gives them a number. Individuality is pushed aside in the name of the country. It seems that God is ignoring them. That is painful and frightening. When I meet someone whose life has been devastated like that, I feel pushed away. I have no courage to ask God why these things happen."

The old train was jolting along on its journey. At this hour on a Sunday, the other passengers were sitting quietly, wrapped in their own thoughts. They did not seem to take any special notice of us. Many dozed in their seats in response to the vibrations of the train. I tried to comfort my friend.

"You are giving these patients physical comfort," I said.

"How much does it help those who are facing such a wretched fate? My prayers, my songs, they seem like tricks or terrible hypocrisy. I feel like beating myself up."

"Don't despair," I said.

He wept. "What do you mean 'despair'? It's a luxury for anyone to despair. It's an escape for those of us who have a normal body, but they have no room for despair. I don't understand why they have to bear this burden while they are bedridden. I really don't know."

I found myself feeling very small, as if I were stuck between two huge mountains named Anguish and—a new one encountered today—Endless Sorrow.

A page of Mang Eui-Soon's sermon notes

Karl Holl 曰「一切의 宗敎에서는 自身을 尊敬하고, 그리고 尊敬할만하고 敎養있고 非難할데 없는 人物들을 그 宗敎交際에 받아드리는데, 基督敎는 도당의 문지를 틀어보냈다. 조금도 罪를 犯하지 안으면 ~~도리어~~ 아주 이상스러운 일인거나 같이! 基督敎의 神은 그의 주위에 罪人들만 모아 놓고 있는 도적놈들의 괴수와 같이, ―― 그렇다. 희랍人이나 로-마人들은 侮辱한者였다면, 神께서 말씀하시는 것은 거룩하고 의심할수 없는 信仰의 理致다」

참으로 十字架를 말함은 하나님을 冒瀆하는 일이오, 不敬虔하기 짝이 없는 無神論者의 毒言이다. 참으로 그렇다. 逆說이오, 容納할수 없는 일이다. 바울과 其他 使徒들이 其當時 敬虔하고 敎養있는 宗敎家들에게 얼마나 핍박과 미움을 받았는가?

참으로 基督敎人들은 反動이다.

하나님이 사람이 되어 人生 속으로 오셨습니다. 그리하여 罪人을 사랑하시다가 十字架에서 돌아가셨다.

「神은 敗北로, 無關心한 이 世上에 神은 그 사랑을 갖이 오셨나니

神을 求해도「神에 있어도 自己만을 爲해 求하는 人生」

이 神人의 앎을 헐뜯던 人生의 自我的 生活을 그치고, 神愛에 의하여 몸을 매는 방법의 方法. 그렇나, 神과 利己主義―의 두 世界 사이의 深淵. 人生이 좇지 않으니 神이 代理的 희생(犧牲)을 當하셨다.

自我的 人生生活이 神愛에 適合하기를 拒絶하여도, 神愛는 自我的 人生生活의 制限에 適合하기를 拒絶하지 않는다.

神愛는 自己 追求에 自身을 주는데 저주하지 않는다.

人生의 自己追求의 犧牲이 된 사랑 (神은 罪를 이기지 못하는 者를 우리 代身 罪로 定하사 우리로 하여 그안에서 義롭다 함을 얻게 하셨나니라)

神의 愛는 永遠한 짝 사랑이다.

PART TWO
How Long, Oh Lord?

The Communists Strike South

On the dull and rainy Sunday morning of June 25, 1950, people were taking the opportunity to sleep in. The heavy rain signaled the start of the monsoon season. For some, this was cause for grumbling, but for others, there was optimism for prolific rice crops. Most of the 1.5 million citizens of Seoul were expecting a quiet day of rest. But the Christians going to church for Sunday worship were anxious because of rumors circulating around the city—rumors that the North Koreans had invaded the South, crossing the thirty-eighth parallel.

There was talk back and forth. “We’ve heard these rumors before, but this time it may be serious.”

“Don’t worry too much; worry invites calamity.”

“Will God spare us a catastrophe? We have enough misery.”

Just weeks earlier, on June 8, North Korea put a statement in its newspaper from the Central Committee of the Unification of Fatherland Democratic Front. The ultimate objective of this action was to implement a call for a general election on the unification of North and South Korea by August 15, 1950, the fifth anniversary of Korean independence. Many people ignored this tactic as stereotypical Communist propaganda, but others saw it as a warning. They quoted a Korean maxim, "If something is mentioned often enough, something serious will happen."

As the international political situation developed in precarious directions, people were afraid that the blast of gunshots from afar might signal local fighting. The government of China collapsed after Generalissimo Chiang Kai-Shek and his army left the mainland. The Communists in China then took control of the mainland. Unsettled situations in Czechoslovakia and Berlin were ominous, and the Indochina war, stirred up by the Communists, forecast a bleak future. Parallel to this international strife, the fighting, murder, and destruction continued in a divided country. Neither pessimists nor optimists could predict the future.

Mang Eui-Soon awoke to the rain, knelt down, and meditated as usual. Quietly, so that he did not disturb his father and stepmother, he made preparations for the outing he had planned for that day. As if hearing his thoughts, his stepmother knocked softly on the door to his room. "You should have something to eat," she said. "You might miss lunch going to Bupyung."

The roasted soy and rice cakes tasted sweet and cool. "Where did you get this?" Mang Eui-Soon asked. "Save it for the two of you. When I go to church, I will have lots of chances to eat delicious snacks. Still, everything is very tasty."

Outside, the rain fell heavily, but inside, all was cozy. He was happy. How could this compare with anything else?

Warm tears welled up. "Mom," he repeated, "I think I am too spoiled."

"God has granted you this happiness," she responded, "and we thank him for you."

After devotions at predawn and a visit to Severance Hospital with four or five of the middle-school students from his church, Mang Eui-Soon came back with them for worship. The rain had cleared, and the morning sun made everything glisten.

But around ten, the ground began to shake. Army jeeps sped around the city with microphones blaring, "Soldiers, return to your company immediately!" The people, enjoying the summer Sunday morning, only briefly wondered what was happening as they continued their outings to churches, palaces, riversides, theaters, and department stores.

The students, however, were shaken by the news. "Mr. Mang," they said, "the situation seems serious. This time, it won't be just a local war."

Park Yong-Ki, a high school senior and president of the church student council, spoke with great anxiety. "For a while, South Korea was too arrogant. Rather than embracing her independence with humility and thankfulness, we ruthlessly oppressed others and murdered so many. Now we deserve punishment."

Another student disagreed. "Why should the South be punished? It was the Communists who disturbed the South."

Park Yong-Ki retorted, "Were our troubles initiated by them? Was it the Communists who killed our patriots, the ones who risked their lives for our independence and freedom? Mr. Mang, what do you think?"

Mang Eui-Soon said nothing for a moment. Then he said, "There are many who made mistakes. There are many politicians and businessmen who work only for their own interests while pretending to be patriotic. Because they desire power, they try to get rid of people who are against them. They ruin others to get money for themselves. But we have to win our own battle. We should live victorious lives every day. Victory means to stand on God's side. It means living every day as if it were our last. We cannot afford to look at the mistakes of others and get angry. And we cannot pray to avoid punishment, because we cannot change God's plans. But we should pray to remain true to God's precepts, even in times of trial and suffering."

While some continued debating the political situation, others were happily excited about their picnic plans. One first-year high-school girl said to Mang Eui-Soon, "This morning I complained about the weather spoiling our picnic plans, but now it has cleared. I was awake all night preparing food. Mr. Mang, please finish the Bupyung service as quickly as possible and join us."

But Mang Eui-Soon said he would not be able to attend the picnic. "I will be quick enough in Bupyung, however, so I can catch up with you for the evening service of praise. Since the picnic is already planned, you should go ahead with it, but I suggest you offer a few moments of prayer for the many young people at the thirty-eighth parallel who are being injured or even killed in battle. We are indebted to them that we can gather here and worship together. Behave well today. Meditate on the cross of Christ, and remember those engaged in war at the front."

The day shone brilliantly after the rain. The sky was a crystal blue, and the new leaves on the trees breathed freshness into the air. During the worship service, the choir filled the church with its songs of praise. People one after another knelt humbly in prayer.

What a contrast to the chaos Mang Eui-Soon experienced at the Seoul station on his way to Bupyung! The loudspeakers on the army vehicle blared out that soldiers should return immediately to their barracks. Radios blasted the same urgent message. Soldiers were running. Grim-faced officials sped back to their offices. Boys delivering the daily newspaper shouted, "Extra! Extra!" and people rushed to pick up a copy of the paper. In it they read, "At four o'clock this morning, North Korean communists invaded the South through the thirty-eighth parallel. Our men are confronting and expelling them." Another army truck rolled by, shouting for soldiers to return to their base.

Soldiers and officers were swarming into the Seoul train station. Some soldiers took a tramcar in the direction of Chungyangri, while others tramped restlessly looking for shortcuts back to their barracks. Mang Eui-Soon closed his eyes while waiting for his train and prayed fervently, "Lord, what has happened? Father, what is waiting for us? For what and how should we prepare?"

False News from the Government

The clear sky turned overcast by afternoon. At Bupyung Army Hospital things were quiet, as if no one knew about the war.

A group of volunteers from the Patriotic Women's Association were chatting, wrapping gauze, and cutting cotton balls. Mang Eui-Soon entered the room in the hospital reserved for worship and saw Yu Chung-In. As she looked at him with her big dark eyes, she smiled and said, "You made it! How is Seoul?"

"Soldiers are being called back to duty. On my way here, I saw them returning to their barracks. A lot depends on how strong the attack is. Have you heard any new developments?"

"It seems that north of Kaesong, Dongdoochun and the east front were attacked all at once. The radio said our soldiers are doing well and we should not have to move. We are winning."

"Well, are we winning really? I'm not sure that's true, considering the situation in Seoul where we are under attack."

"Mr. Mang, don't be too pessimistic. We have the power to resist any attack," she said trying to console him, but her face showed her deep worry. She could not hide the ominous and oppressive feelings she experienced when she heard the morning news report on the outbreak of war.

After the service, they worked at the intensive care unit for a while. As he made his rounds, Mang asked, "Were you told what to do in case of a war situation? If an emergency arises, we may be affected here at the hospital."

"Well, so far we haven't gotten any orders. That indicates to me that every thing is still all right."

"If something happens, we'll have to do a lot here. The critical patients will have to be moved." Seeing Yu's grim face, Mang Eui-Soon tried to cheer her up by saying, "I think our worries may be unfounded. I hope nothing serious happens. If so, I would come immediately to help you."

"Will you have dinner here tonight?"

"Not now. I am worried about Seoul, so I must leave now. I will see you next Sunday. If anything happens, I will come right away."

But Mang Eui-Soon had an unshakable premonition of disaster as he stood there. Their eyes met. "Take care of yourself," they whispered to each other.

When Mang Eui-Soon returned to Seoul, the city seemed quieter, but Mang Eui-Soon watched as panic-stricken American families packed their luggage and rushed in their cars toward Noryangjin, a suburb. They did not want to get hurt while we were shooting and killing each other and trampling our own people under our feet. We, however, had nowhere else to go.

The streets had lost their usual vitality. An occasional army or civilian truck sped by, packed with soldiers. People who had come out to enjoy the holiday hurried home. Some church members were reluctant to leave the evening service and tried to encourage each other. One said, "War seems to have broken out, but hopefully it will turn out well for us. We must take this as an opportunity to show our strength for unification." Another agreed, "Yes, we have often said that if and when the North regime provokes us, we will capture Pyongyang and liberate the people there." Everyone wanted to believe that.

Mang Eui-Soon joined people hurrying to get home. A plane flew overhead. "An enemy airplane! It's a Russian reconnaissance plane!" This left everyone unsettled and worried as they scurried home.

Elder Mang was listening to the radio when Mang Eui-Soon got home. "The North is waging a full-scale war. They have attacked, starting at Ongjin, then Kaesong, Jangdan, Dongdoochun, Pochun, Choonchun, and Kangnung. They landed from ships on the east coast. Even though the radio says that our men are quickly expelling the enemy, we are being defeated at Dongdoochun. Maybe we are all right. We must trust our military forces," his father told him.

Father and son sat with their ears tuned to the radio. "At Ongjin, we captured tanks, rifles, muskets, machine guns, and cannons. We destroyed one Communist battalion. A Communist regimental commander voluntarily surrendered along with his regiment. Details of numbers of soldiers and their names will be announced when we have them. We have sunk an armed enemy warship that landed on the east coast."

Mang Eui-Soon's father heaved a sigh of relief. "That's not bad. Our men have endured hardships, but they also have fought off an assault and shouldn't suffer too much harm. Taking into account our competence, we might even end the war soon. It will be good if we can achieve unification by taking advantage of this opportunity, although we will suffer some losses. We could then visit our forsaken hometown."

Mang Eui-Soon withdrew to his room but could not sleep. The darkness slipped away, and daybreak came as Mang Eui-Soon headed to the morning worship service. He found a few army vehicles at Severance Hospital, unloading wounded soldiers. Some staggered down from the vehicles on their own, but the seriously injured lay unconscious, bleeding profusely despite the bandages wrapped around their hands, legs, shoulders, and eyes. He began to help carry them into the hospital. Doctors and nurses, who had been called in at night, checked the patients quickly, but there were so many patients that they could not care for all of them.

A nurse almost cried, overjoyed at his coming. “Oh, Mr. Mang, thank you for coming. Surely God cares about us.”

The wounded soldiers cried out, “The Russian T34 tanks are horrifying and devastating! We cannot hold them back!”

“We don’t have tanks. We don’t have even mines to destroy tanks,” said others.

“It’s not just tanks we are lacking,” grumbled an officer whose uniform pants had been torn into strips to wrap his injured leg. “We only have a few cannons. The enemy is equipped with tanks that shoot with precision. If we had such equipment, we would not have suffered such a loss.” He seemed more concerned with equipment than his injury.

A soldier lying on a blanket in the corridor cried out, “Give us tanks—tanks and cannons! I can go to the front . . . even now. My friends were killed. They died right beside me.”

“We are struggling with a few M1 rifles. We have some mortars and light machine guns, but they are in short supply. We were deceived, blackmailed!” Other wounded soldiers, sprawled in the corridor, groaned in agreement.

In October 1945, the year of Korean independence, the National Defense Headquarters was established. The following January, the National Defense Battalion (which later became the ROK Army) was formed, designed by the United States. It became known as the poorest attempt at military logistics in Korean history. No military equipment was stockpiled, and the scarcity of commodities forced them to import US surplus agricultural products rather than military supplies. The priority was daily food and clothes and commodities. All vehicles were mobilized for food transport, so there was no time or money for military preparation. Furthermore, the US forces stationed in Korea, as well as the US government, concluded that Korean affairs were a recurring nuisance and so made no contingency plans.[1]

During the Second World War, the United States misjudged its ally Russia. By assuming Russia's good intentions, by not analyzing the current situation critically, and by not looking to the future, the United States blundered greatly and helped bring about a tragic outcome in Korean history.[2] To the United States, the Korean army was like a ragged bundle carried by a stranger in whom they had no interest at all.

When the US secretary of state, John Foster Dulles, visited the front, he said the United States would continue to give economic aid for the democracy of Korea, but he stated with an ill-advised confidence that there was no danger of war. He was briefed about what weapons the Korean army had. He was told that eight divisions in the ROK Army were equipped with M1 rifles, while guerrilla combat teams had only outdated Japanese rifles. The United States supplied machine guns and mortars, but the field artillery defending the infantry divisions had outdated M-3 howitzers. But to the Koreans' chagrin, there were no tanks, no medium-distance cannons, no 4.2-inch mortars, no recoilless guns, and no spare parts for army vehicles. Airplanes were not even considered.

1. Joseph C. Goulden, *Korea: The Untold Story of the War* (New York: Times Books, 1982), pp. 30–2; Max Hastings, *The Korean War* (London: Pan Books, Ltd., 1988), pp. 35–6, 43, 45–7.
2. Ibid., pp. 16–8.

The United States wanted to take advantage of Korea while maintaining popularity in the international arena. John Foster Dulles stated, "Under United States care, the security of Korea is assured. No worry at all."[3]

The Korean Military Advisory Group (KMAG) and the US Department of Defense controlling the KMAG orchestrated the same rhetoric. Two weeks after Dulles left declaring there was "no danger of war in Korea," and even before he arrived in the States carrying that report, the thirty-eighth parallel collapsed miserably. The young and passionate South Korean soldiers who had welcomed Dulles with genuine smiles when he visited the front were now wiped out by the barrage of enemy artillery.[4]

More wounded soldiers came in as day broke. Mang Eui-Soon stayed to help care for the wounded, under the direction of nurses and doctors. An early morning radio message by John Muccio, the US ambassador to Korea, came in. "We spent a day in excitement and tension. But Korean soldiers are doing their best to defend freedom and independence. The status and position of the Korean army this morning became strengthened and it is doing much better compared to last night. The ROK army is praised nationally and internationally for its bravery and excellence. I believe that the righteous purpose of the Korean people will be achieved. The trial is surprising and painful, but important and precious. I am sure that the brave struggle of Koreans will overcome hardship and attain victory.

3. Goulden, pp. 34, 53.
4. Ibid., pp. 37–41.

We are united and will fulfill our duty as individuals or as a team until we attain victory."[5]

Everyone was glued to the radio for news. Those who listened to the radio felt relieved and thought that we were not alone as long as the United States was concerned with our affairs. The Korean Military Press Department announced, "In the battle in Ongjin area our Seventeenth Regiment captured Haejoo City, and our army around the thirty-eighth parallel is advancing twenty kilometers north of the border." But there was no mention of the Kaesong and Yeonbaek areas.

"Maybe they are all right, since we are doing well in Ongjin and other areas, too," one person commented.

But on his way from the hospital to visit the school, Mang Eui-Soon could see how different things were in the areas of Namdaemun and the Seoul railroad station. People were behaving like refugees, moving toward the Han River to the south. Their usual white robes were dusted with yellowish clay. Some women had bundles on their heads. The radio spread good news, but what had happened to these people?

An old farmer was walking a cow. Mang Eui-Soon approached him and asked, "What is going on?"

"I don't know. Yesterday, I was working in the field. Suddenly bullets rained all around me, and I hid on the edge of the field until there was a lull in the shelling. Then I took the cow and walked here."

"Where is your family?" Mang Eui-Soon asked him. "Where are you going?"

---

5. John J. Muccio, interview by Richard D. McKinzie, http://www.trumanlibrary.org/oralhist/muccio3.htm, December 7, 1973.

"I don't know. I just came up here. I am humiliated. I ran away by myself not knowing the whereabouts of my wife and children."

"Is the war situation that serious? The radio reported that everything was okay."

"We are suffering heavy losses. It's like lightning bolts striking in a clear sky."

People passed by them in a hurry without paying attention to their conversation. "If you don't have a destination, what will you do now?" Mang Eui-Soon asked.

"I don't know," the man repeated. "I just ran away to escape death."

The situation at the school was not much different. Both professors and students were panic stricken and flocked from one place to another. Mang told his classmates and junior students that urgent tasks awaited them in the hospital. "Wounded soldiers are flooding the hospital. Doctors and nurses are working hard without breaks. We should go there to help them. Standing here and doing nothing is making us despondent and miserable. Let's go up there."

Just as they were leaving the school for the hospital, one of them shouted, "Look overhead! An enemy airplane!"

Suddenly Mang shouted, "Those are Russian YAK fighter airplanes. Look, there is another one over there! Move back inside!"

One student complained, "Why haven't we heard any warning sirens? Haven't the authorities noticed those planes overhead?"

Bullets strafed the ground as the airplanes flew toward Yongsan, obscuring the midday sun. Another student shouted in exasperation, "Our antiaircraft guns are being fired at!" They could see one of their own airplanes in the sky, but it seemed ineffective against the two Russian planes. "That is just our training airplane," the student said. "How can we compete against them?"

The enemy planes invading Seoul flew over the city, meeting no resistance. Leaflets were dropped as they flew over the navy headquarters of the Yongsan barracks near the government office building called Central Hall. The students walked in despair toward Severance Hospital.

Mang glanced at the sky over Bupyung. "How is it over there?" he wondered. "Can they handle immobilized patients in the face of such a grim situation? Captain Yu might be back home by now because she lives at Sangdo-Dong Neighborhood, but what is she going to do?"

They saw a woman setting a table under the eaves of her small store while listening to the radio. "What does it say?" a student asked her.

She glanced at him and smiled. "We are doing well. A division recaptured the Euichungbu area and routed fifteen thousand of the enemy. Not only that, but they also destroyed more than fifty-eight tanks. Those ******** who brought in their arsenals are now deserting, fleeing us. War has already broken out. I hope the thirty-eighth parallel becomes totally broken, and we take advantage of this chance." In incredulous silence, the students left this naive woman and moved on toward the hospital.

The scene at the hospital entrance was unbearable to witness. A car rushed in, packed with mutilated soldiers, limbs torn apart, bodies covered in blood. Mang Eui-Soon and those with him looked on in horror. "Take the wounded into the emergency room," he ordered. "Find some blankets in the hospital and bring them here. Turn around and move this man into . . ."

"He's dead," someone sighed faintly. The man's body was still warm and lay peacefully on the ground. The shrapnel had passed through him, and blood was pouring out of his body.

Mang Eui-Soon laid him to one side and knelt before him. Maybe he was lucky to be dead rather than having to suffer like those who were still alive. He prayed, "Lord, I entrust his soul to your hands." Tears welled up in Mang Eui-Soon's eyes, and his heart sank. "Whose son are you? You are the eye of your mother. You are the fortress of your father. You are the beloved son, brother, and a pillar for your family, and the starlight hidden in the heart of your lover."

Mang Eui-Soon had little time to mourn. A nurse who knew him grabbed him. "Mr. Mang, Mr. Mang!" she repeated in an urgent tone. "We badly need help. I am so glad you are here."

When he finally arrived home that night, Mang Eui-Soon found his father listening intently, as before, to the radio news. "Dad, I think they are spreading false news. It still reports things favorably for us, but the reality is very different."

"No, Son, we should still believe them. We must trust them. What would happen if people didn't trust their government? In this time of hardship we must trust and stay united and help others. What can the government do if the people do not trust it? Never say that!"

"Dad, I saw a mass of humanity fleeing near Namdaemun, the Seoul railroad station, and on the road to Yongsan.

The area of Chungyangri was clogged with refugees from Euichungbu."

"They are impatient. People following the government directive are true citizens."

The son looked up at his father in silence. Despite a big, strong bone structure and broad features, Elder Mang possessed a meek heart. "Because we have our own government, we are protected and can have a good night's sleep. They are human beings, and sometimes they can make mistakes. If we blame and criticize them every time, how can they rule the country? We have to trust our government."

"Yes, Dad. I am working at the hospital, and I might not come home tomorrow. Don't worry about me, and don't wait up for me."

Dark clouds settled over the hospital where the will to live and the stillness of death coexisted. Doctors and nurses who had gone sleepless for two days were like machines. Accumulated fatigue and the grim reality they constantly faced deprived them of emotion. Their eyes were bloodshot and their lips were chapped. By midnight of the next day, June 26, many soldiers had died after undergoing surgery. Others died where they were, lying in corners and on the sides of the room.

Mang Eui-Soon took a soldier who had been shot in the abdomen from the truck and hurried him to surgery. His heart ached for him as he carried him and laid him in a bed in the corridor. The soldier grabbed Mang Eui-Soon's sleeve and cried, "Please don't go away. Stay with me." His eyes were as black and pure as a deer's as he stared into the air and muttered, "Mo . . . Mom, Mom."

Mang Eui-Soon held his hands as the soldier whispered, "I am afraid and so sad. Those people who shot me and killed my friend used the same language as ours. They looked like me." He began to cry as the soldier continued. "My friend, I left him in the field. The corn and beans were growing where he lay down. I should be there with him."

"I know. I know what it meant to you. Please do not talk. First have the surgery, and when you are recovered, we can talk more."

The soldier nodded, pressed Mang Eui-Soon's hand, and closed his eyes, calling for his mother and his friend still lying in the field. Mang Eui-Soon knelt down by his bed. He could still feel the soldier's warmth. But he could not pray. He should have prayed, "Lord, embrace his soul," but he couldn't. He wondered if the lingering, thin smile on the soldier's dry lips meant that his soul had met his mother.

He had to leave him to report the death immediately. The empty bed was needed for others. Once a person died, he was counted as a casualty. Priority needed to be given to those still alive. The dead bodies were moved out, one by one, without pause or hesitation. Mang Eui-Soon thought, *A body is meaningless and ugly when breathing stops. Why does God have us look at this separation of body from life?* His questioning became desperate. He was exhausted and unable to move.

At six o'clock in the morning of June 27, 1950, the tone of the news drastically changed. No longer were we winning the war. The government decided to move the capital to Suwon temporarily because the surrounding area of Seoul was under enemy control. There were no directions for the people about what to do. The same news was reported over and over.

"No, how could it be?" people asked, feeling betrayed and shattered. "Could we not resist for three days? What should we do?"

Even at the hospital, there were no directives or special information given. Some officials and soldiers in charge of transporting the wounded took care of them. Mang Eui-Soon watched from a hospital window as masses of people passed through the Seoul railroad station. Amplifying the chaos, the shrieking of cannons and missiles resonated nearer and nearer. People were fleeing south to escape the cannon fire. The Yongsan area leading to the Han River was jammed with waves of humanity. Cars crowded the roads. Army trucks carried wounded soldiers. Trucks were packed tight with refugees. Vehicles were camouflaged with branches. But the cars rolled at the same speed as the walkers. How could they leave their homes that easily, abandoning everything they knew and loved? Where were they going? What awaited them? Would the government be able to establish itself at Suwon?

The trucks kept bringing in the wounded soldiers, bleeding and crying in agony. Then a voice in the crowd shouted, "The Euichungbu resistance line has collapsed. We are trapped. We are fighting with our bare hands. We don't have enough hand grenades. If I had some, I would throw myself at a tank. My friend did that and disappeared in a blast. But we don't have hand grenades, so we climb over the tanks and fight, smashing them with hammers and axes under a barrage of machine-gun fire."

And still, the radio continued to send news that Euichungbu was recaptured, giving false solace to our agony. Nurses in army fatigues shouted the news, "Euichungbu is recaptured. Euichungbu is recaptured." Through the streams of refugees, someone posted the news on the walls to inform the people. But the sound of cannons came closer and closer.

"Isn't that strange, that we are hearing the cannons grow louder and louder when Euichungbu has been recaptured?" someone said.

People felt confused and couldn't decide whether to retreat or not. Around three thirty in the afternoon, the radio finally announced good news. "Tomorrow morning, June 28, at eight o'clock, US forces will join the war. A war office has been formed in General MacArthur's headquarters, and the operation is under way."

While Mang Eui-Soon listened to the news, he felt relieved, but then he suddenly thought: *What stupid mentality was this? Why should we take it for granted that the United States will help us? Who will be the target, and who will be killed? And who are the ones invading from the North, ruthlessly slaughtering and devastating this land? My face looks like theirs. We are brothers, sharing the same blood; but they are getting weapons from Russia and engaging in ruthless killing. Why are people in this land bringing in foreign soldiers to kill our people in order to govern us? This is a strange and shameful country.*

A long time ago the Korean Peninsula had boasted a unified Silla kingdom, but this unification was attained through the military intervention of Tang China. Four hundred years later the Koryo kingdom faced the threat of invasion by the Mongols. There was a difference of opinion about how to deal with this threat. The position of the patriotic army, called Sambyulcho, insisted on resistance. The government sought a peace treaty with the Mongols that effectively gave them control of the country. How did the government handle itself in the face of the Mongol invasion? They crushed the Sambyulcho army, effectively inviting the Mongols to take control of the country.[6]

Another shameful aspect of Korean history is how the followers of the Tonghak (Eastern Learning) movement were treated. This native religious movement attempted to bring about political reform and social justice, minimizing the foreign influences and enhancing the qualities of the common people. The corrupt government of the Yi dynasty (Choson kingdom) invited the Japanese and Chinese armies to halt the spread of the Tonghak insurgents, resulting in crushing and beating down its own people using foreign troops.[7]

Mang Eui-Soon realized that in order to control Korea, the North had brought in the Russians to invade and kill the Korean people, and the South was looking to the United States for help and security. With the United States joining the war, Mang Eui-Soon wondered what fate lay ahead for his land, his country. "What will happen to us, if we take things so carelessly and do not learn the lessons of the past? Even more, what is my role, and how should I fulfill it?"

---

6. Ki-Baik Lee, *A New History of Korea*, translated by Edward W. Wagner with Edward J. Shultz (Harvard University Press, 1984), pp. 66–7, 151, 283–90.
7. Ibid.

Seoul in Turmoil

As darkness approached, it began to drizzle. Cannons roared nearby. Despite the rain and darkness, refugees continued to pour onto the roads. On one side of the hospital, the bodies of the dead piled up. Because of the shortage of workers, it was almost impossible to take in the increasing number of wounded soldiers. What was worse was that there were still no directives from the authorities.

Mang Eui-Soon worried about his family. What should he do? Should he be at home with his parents? Should he tell them to flee south? Mang Eui-Soon talked with an army surgeon and a major in charge of transport. "I would like to see my parents for a little while and come back early tomorrow morning."

The surgeon smiled and patted him on the back and said, "You have done ten times more than what we have done. I know you are worried about your family. Your dedication and attitude assured me that there is a future for our country. I have a little time now and will take you in my car because it is raining so heavily." He glanced at his watch. It was past one o'clock in the morning.

The major urged Mang Eui-Soon into his jeep. Heavy rain pounded down on the stream of refugees. The major left the entrance of Severance Hospital, but the jeep could not get through the lines of people. Mang Eui-Soon said, "I will get out. It will be much faster."

The major turned on the flashlight, glanced at his watch, and nodded. With his flashlight he illuminated Mang Eui-Soon's face. "We couldn't look each other in the face because we were so rushed with work. Ah, the face of Korea, the face of conscience. Thank you."

The heavy showers quickly drenched Mang Eui-Soon. He walked slowly, pushing his way forward as if he were swimming. Endless lines of refugees moved along in a cacophony of vocal despair. They had no final destination but single-mindedly wanted to cross the Han River. He hurried home. Elder Mang and his wife sat in the lamplight in a corner, listening to the radio.

"Oh, my dear, you are soaked from the rain," his stepmother said, delighted at his return. "Wash and dry yourself with a towel." As she poured water over the basin from the cistern, she said, "The United States has joined the war reluctantly."

The three family members sat quietly. Finally Elder Mang asked, "Are there many refugees on the road?"

"Yes, Dad. They are clogging the road, despite the rain."

"What will happen?"

"I don't know. The situation is unpredictable. I think our countrymen have forgotten one thing that we must do. "

"What's that?"

"Think about why we are in this miserable situation. Everyone is struggling to survive by running away, but nobody dares to think why we are in this situation. It reminds me of the words from Jeremiah 4: 'Break up your fallow ground, and sow not among thorns. Circumcise yourselves to the LORD, remove the foreskin of your hearts . . . lest my wrath go forth like fire, and burn with none to quench it, because of the evil of your doings.'"

His father closed his eyes and said nothing. The sound of rain was all that broke the silence.

Suddenly, a tremendous din of explosions shook the ground. The three of them caught their breath together. A bomb drop? An atomic bomb, even? Another explosion and then silence and more rain.

"It sounded like a bomb, but I could not tell for sure," said Elder Mang, irritated. "The world will end like that! Get some sleep, Son. You look tired. I don't think anything else will happen until dawn."

Mang went to his room and lay on the floor, but he felt suffocated by the rain and the roar of artillery fire. The last two days had been like an eternal hell. Afraid to sleep, he also longed to forget everything in sleep. Finally, exhausted, he fell asleep.

He awoke to brilliant sunlight shining through the window. Guiltily, he sprang from the floor. "I did not wake you up because you were so exhausted," said Kwonsa La, hesitantly.

The storm clouds had disappeared completely. The gunfire had stopped. The crystal clear sky revealed a tranquility that subdued all the cruel sounds of war.

"Oh, the hospital! . . . I slept too long. How is Dad?"

"He fell asleep a moment ago. I want him to sleep because he needs it. For some unknown reason, the radio broadcasting has stopped. It seems that the enemy troops have retreated."

"Maybe," said Mang Eui-Soon.

He walked briskly toward the hospital, feeling sorry for those who had worked all night. But suddenly he was afraid. Strange tanks plastered with yellow mud stains were rolling toward the Yungchun Dongripmoon (Independence Gate), their noisy engines numbing the ears. The tank hatches were open, and inside strange soldiers dressed in mustard-colored uniforms were aiming their machine guns outside. People lining the streets were waving hastily made red flags. *What are these people doing here?* thought Mang Eui-Soon, momentarily paralyzed.

He saw a neighbor walking by, looking exhausted, with his two young sons. He hurried with them into an alley. The old man whispered in tears, "Last night we tried to leave. Just past midnight, the bridge over the Han River was blown out. It was said that our own army did that for tactical reasons, but many refugees were killed by the blast or drowned when they fell into the river. At daybreak, we returned home, only to find Seoul was already in the hands of the enemy. My wife and I came home separately in case we were found fleeing and the enemy killed us. We are doomed to death! Please don't walk around. Hide somewhere."

Mang Eui-Soon hurried back home. Elder Mang was now awake and had heard the radio announcement that Seoul was under control of the enemy. "What curse has come upon us?" he cried in panic.

"Dad, the street is now lined with Communist tanks. I saw civilians waving red flags. The explosion last night came when the Han River Bridge was demolished."

Making up his mind to return to the hospital, Mang Eui-Soon felt helplessness overwhelm him as he walked along the street. The crispness of the air washed by rains seemed to exist without purpose. Thunderous tanks rolled by, and the fluttering red flags appeared to be a mirage. Neither rampant joy nor lamentable despair welcomed the tanks. It was more like complete confusion. Seoul was now like a closed, devastated city. The government had fooled the people by saying everything was all right, and then the leaders had run away with their own possessions, abandoning their citizens. On Monday, June 26, 1950, the Korean president, Rhee Syngman, decided to abandon Seoul because he thought that his army could not hold Seoul anymore. The decision touched off angry debate in the national assembly. After an hour-long debate, the assembly voted, and the decision was made that the majority would stay in Seoul with the people. Late on Monday night the president's staff assembled two special trains to carry him, his chief advisers, and their families south away from the battle. The majority of members of the national assembly who had voted only hours earlier to remain in Seoul, regardless of the Communist advance, had fled south across the Han River.[8]

When the people tried to follow after the assembly members, the panicked ROK forces prematurely blew out the bridge over the Han River to delay the advance of the North Koreans.[9] The citizens of Seoul were entrapped on June 28, 1950, without any knowledge of what was going on. Overnight, their world had changed.

Mang Eui-Soon hurried toward the Seoul railroad station. Although they were the enemy, he thought, they are still human. *If we ask them for help for the wounded, they might give us some special allowance.* With this hope, he felt a new determination.

Passing the Yumchung Bridge, he met a panicked nurse. "Where are you going, Mr. Mang? Don't go to the

8. Goulden, pp. 71, 79.
9. Ibid, p. 89.

hospital if that's what you are intending. We must escape immediately."

"What happened?" he asked, dismayed that he had slept in.

"They've occupied the hospital. I went home before dawn for a break and went back to the hospital a moment ago. They were dragging our wounded soldiers out into the backyard to shoot them! Oh God . . ." Overwhelmed with tears, she could not finish. Mang Eui-Soon started to leave her to head toward the hospital, but she hung on to him. "It's useless. Even if you go there, they won't listen to you. If you go there, your life will end with a gunshot. Don't go, please. Trust me."

"I have to see for myself."

"Then I will go with you."

After crossing at the Seoul railroad station, they followed a hill and hid in the bushes. The trees were fresh after the overnight rains, and everything could be clearly seen in the sunlight. Behind the tile-roofed houses, they could see Severance Hospital. They saw soldiers dressed in drab, mustard-colored uniforms pulling out the wounded, dragging or pushing them out, and throwing them beside a wall.

"Soon we will hear shots. And it will be over," she said.

"Aren't they going to treat them as POWs? How could this happen?"

"To the Communists the wounded are a nuisance. It would be a headache to feed and care for them as POWs. They might need the hospital to accommodate their own men. The staff who spent three straight nights there were sent home for a break, but the others remained there without any choice in the matter."

"What will happen to them?"

"They will be kept under watch."

"How terrible it is for all of them."

"Yes, especially on this brilliant morning."

"Ah, why is the sky so blue . . . why the sun so dazzling?" thought both Mang and the nurse. Her whole body shaking, the nurse held Mang's hands in her own as she said goodbye.

On the street, everything was becoming even more chaotic. Civilians were being forced onto the street without knowing why and made to lift their hands and shout "Hurrah," fearing the consequences if they refused. Continuing down through the street were the growling tanks, cannons, howitzers, and guns of the occupiers.

"How can we survive?" he said to himself. "Survive, what does that mean? To live?" He thought about his mother, his older sister, his older brother, and his younger sister—all dead. Suddenly it occurred to him that they might be lucky. To be alive meant to suffer and to continue to suffer. *Why am I alive,* thought Mang, *if only to suffer? What awaits me?* He lifted up his head, looking into the sky.

Hiding on Chungnung Mountain

The sun was blazing and the earth was dry and dusty as Mang Eui-Soon climbed Chungnung Mountain near Seoul. Reverend Bae from Namdaemun Church climbed with him. They were searching for a safe place deep in the mountains to avoid capture by the Communists. Shade from the trees offered little respite from the sun.

"I cannot go on anymore. Let's take a rest and have some water," said a pale Reverend Bae. While pouring water, Mang Eui-Soon looked at his hands and laughed bitterly, remembering his stepmother and what she had said in their last moments together. "Rub your hands, both the back and palm with dirt. When the soldiers catch people, they first examine the hands to see whether they are laborers or not." Then she had rubbed the backs and palms of his hands mercilessly with coarse sand.

The four then had held a worship service. As Reverend Bae and Mang Eui-Soon were leaving, the elder Mang had looked at his son with a deep sadness. "Continue to pray to seek courage and wisdom. God is with you," he had said, his eyes filled with compassion.

His stepmother's words were: "Pray, whether you are walking, sitting, awaking, or slumbering. Pray constantly. And let the words of the Bible not depart from you. Whatever hardship we may have, it is the will of God. Just give thanks to God, lest you grieve him."

He looked at his rough hands again. "How can my disguised hands fool the Communists? I've never used them for labor." Reverend Bae, exhausted, was asleep against a pine tree. Mang Eui-Soon watched the older man sleep and wondered about him. At forty years of age, he was in the prime of life, but this difficult traveling had tired him so quickly. He had devoted his life to saving souls and not to physical labor either.

He checked to see how much food was left in the bundle he was carrying on his back: a few loaves of wheat bread, some roasted barley powder his stepmom had prepared, some salt, and a few pounds of rice. That was all. How long this would support them? The steamy weather amplified their distress.

Just six days after Seoul had been abandoned, the enemy also captured Suwon, and it had already been a week since the next line of our defense had been established. How far had our government retreated? Communist radio bragged of the imminent liberation of Busan, but our radio announced that the army had retreated. If the government's announcement could be trusted, the enemy was having a hard time in the Suwon battle, but who knew the truth?

In Seoul, starvation was pervasive. The only ones who walked confidently were rifle-carrying Communists and the few collaborators. Grain fields at their peak ready to be harvested were devastated by gunfire and tanks. The war would kill more people by starvation than by bullets and bombs.

At night, they had to worry about the persistent mosquitoes. Mang Eui-Soon wondered, "How can such little suckers enjoy the taste of blood!" Still, this mountain seemed like a paradise compared to hiding under the floor of Hapdong house. There were stars overhead instead of a miasma of fungi penetrating the skin and the piercing smells from the mixture of fungi and sweat.

The Communists had detailed lists of people who had fled to the South before the start of the war in 1950, numbering about two million people. An extensive search was undertaken. In the middle of the nights before he and Reverend Bae set out, enemy soldiers had searched houses, cruelly attacking like nocturnal animals. He and his family had been attacked twice, but they had hidden under the floor and were not discovered. In the darkness at the sound of the army boots trampling above him on the floor, Mang Eui-Soon had felt as if he were in a deep sea of fear, like a man just before drowning. "Why, Lord? What is your will for me? Why do I feel that you are not here? Why do you hide me in the midst of uncountable deaths and destruction? For what purpose am I hiding in this place?"

It had seemed as if time did not exist there. Stuck in a dingy, smelly, damp pit and overtaken by despair, he had said, "God, I am not so much loving you as I am afraid of you. It is said that God works in everything for good with those who love him, those who are called according to his purpose, but what good can this darkness be?"

But now on the mountain, he looked at the stars, a little window through which to see eternity. *If we all could just look up at the stars in the sky three times a night*, he thought, *we wouldn't kill each other.*

He had not encountered any North Korean troops yet, but he assumed that they were not different in the color of their blood or in their feelings, although their ideology was so different from that of the South. They had the same skin color, used the same language, ate the same kimchi and rice, and wore the same kinds of clothes as he did—as they all did. So why should they be playing the role of killers? Are their dying soldiers crying for their mothers?

I am still alive, Mang Eui-Soon thought. *I am still breathing, eating, and looking at the stars in the night sky. But for what purpose? People are being killed, and I am in hiding. Where and how will my life be used? Am I alive to keep the words from Psalm 150: "Let everything that breathes praise the* LORD*"? Is my soul praising the Lord? But how can I praise you, Lord, when*

I think of so many deaths and so much bloodshed? Why have you made me see such devastation? Lying down in despair and crying with clenched fists, he was not able to overcome the darkness that surrounded him, inside and out.

Day one, day two, and day three went by. They seemed to go slowly while the food ran out quickly. Mang Eui-Soon felt pain in his heart for Reverend Bae when he realized that he was grappling with problems of his own. "Accept this as a blessing," Reverend Bae said. "God is testing our people. We have to humble ourselves in the face of suffering. Suffering is a path leading to God's blessings."

"These words are too valuable for me to have all to myself," responded Mang Eui-Soon.

"Well, if God spares me, I will tell them to my congregation. And I believe we will talk about you as a lesson in Christian living, in the future. Here on this mountain we have an opportunity to cry out to the Lord. We have to remember that God brought us here to pray, not to escape the danger."

The nearly empty food bag had held enough for three days. After that they had to survive on just water from the valley. "Reverend Bae, let's go down the mountain," said Mang Eui-Soon.

"How can we go? There are so many guards on the street. Christians are their most detestable enemy. Maybe you can go down south straight from here if you think you should leave. If you penetrate the frontlines and reach the place where our troops are stationed, you will be safe."

Penetrate the front? That was unthinkable, thought Mang Eui-Soon. But just at that moment, they heard shots being fired, breaking the summer silence. The two men stood up, the grass where they had been lying slowly returning to its former state. In the distance they saw Communists walking up the trail, carrying rifles, searching here and there in the bushes to pull out people from hiding places.

"There must be other people hiding on this mountain," said Reverend Bae. Maybe our retreating soldiers from the Miari hill battle have come here."

More gunfire cracked, and they heard the soldiers nearby, shouting orders.

Reverend Bae dropped his head, holding on to a pine tree. As Mang knelt beside him, he prayed, "Lord, what should I ask, how should I pray at the moment? Should I pray to preserve my life, or should I seek your righteousness? God, in this situation, I don't know what is happening to us, but I only seek your will."

Through the trees, Mang and Reverend Bae could see some enemy soldiers dragging captured South Korean soldiers and civilians down the mountain, while others continued to search the ridge and valleys. The two did not move. The water in their bottle had long ago run out, and now their empty stomachs were dry and twisted. Finally the saving darkness of night encompassed them.

They listened as enemy troops walked by them, shouting, "Poke into every crevice, and don't miss those trees!"

Soldiers waded into the bushes, whirling a flashlight that seemed brighter than a searchlight. "Come out with your hands up!"

Reverend Bae and Mang held their breaths. Someone was detected. Pow! Pow! Gunshots pierced the darkness.

"Next it is our turn," whispered Mang as gunfire scattered in all directions, and flashlights were oscillating through the darkness. Their tongues parched and throats choking in thirst, the two lay prostrate beside the trunk of the tree.

Is this the end? Is my last moment to be like this? wondered Mang Eui-Soon. "Lord, forgive my unfaithfulness. Have mercy on me. Be all in me," he prayed. He wept before God for his sense of failure, even as the searchers passed them by, some nearly stepping on them. Soon it was quiet and calm. The searchers were gone, and there was only darkness.

In the Courtyard of the Hyangrinwon Orphanage

The two men slipped away from Chungnung Mountain and made their way back to Hapdong house in Seoul. Seoul was being bombed again. Arriving safely home, they learned that Park Yong-Ki, the president of the church student council, had just left.

Mang Eui-Soon rose immediately to go after him.

Kwonsa La rose after him. "The bombing is rampant," she said. "It isn't safe out there."

"The harder the bombing, the less thorough the search becomes," answered Mang with determination. Reverend Bae agreed and decided to go with him.

The air-raid warning had been lifted, but Seoul seemed paralyzed. As they were crossing the street to Jeodong neighborhood, a bomb from an airplane dropped with no warning, causing the ground to shake from the explosion. Even the sunlight was momentarily blotted out by the thundering explosion. Buildings nearby were shattered and burning. People on the streets ran in all directions, not knowing where to find shelter. Then a voice cried out to them, "Sir, over there; Chang-Hyun has fallen!"

Chang-Hyun had had one arm blown off. Mang Eui-Soon could see it lying on the blood-smeared rubble. Mang threw him over his shoulder, listening for his heartbeat and praying as he ran. The students running with him panted, "This way! There is a clinic!"

They found it already in pandemonium. "We don't have drugs, and we need more doctors," said a nurse, stamping her feet in frustration.

Several students surrounded her and said, "We will provide blood. Give us the names of drugs you need. We will get them from drugstores somehow."

At that moment, the ground shook violently as the bombing started again. Mang Eui-Soon quickly put Chang-Hyun under the bed. "Everyone, on the ground!" he ordered. "And watch for shrapnel!"

While they lay there, Mang Eui-Soon asked the doctor to write the names of the drugs that were needed and to get ready to take blood. "Anyone with type O blood should stay here. The rest of you try to get medicine."

When the airplane disappeared, the students went out to get what medications they could. The doctor returned to work with determination. "You have given me new confidence and faith." Someone said with relief, "Chang-Hyun is alive."

At dawn Park Yong-Ki, Mang Eui-Soon's student from church school, visited him by stealth to escape danger. Soon after this, Mang Eui-Soon and Park Yong-Ki fled to the mountains north of Seoul to avoid capture by the Communists. The terrain was steep. Sweltering under the trees, with heat rising in waves over the rocky earth, they stopped for a break. "Mr. Mang," Park Yong-Ki asked, wiping away his sweat, "why was Reverend Bae so adamant about telling us to flee south?"

"That is the conclusion he came to after prayer."

"Why did you choose to go north instead?"

"In this situation how can we dare go south? We would be easily detected and shot to death."

"You said they were God's words. How can you tell which are God's words?"

"Maybe we will hear his voice while we are going up this mountain."

Park sighed. "I am really confused. The enemy troops are using our church for their stables. Their horses are trampling down our church and relieving themselves there. Chang-Hyun encountered misery and lost his arm when he was going to worship service, and you know his kind heart and his faithfulness. I am really bewildered."

Mang responded by citing Isaiah 55: "For my thoughts are not your thoughts, neither are your ways my ways. . . . For as the heavens are higher than the earth, so are my ways higher than your ways and my thoughts than your thoughts."

"I don't know, sir. Faced with this danger, I can only think of running away. When facing trials, I forget about the cross of Christ entirely. If only we had time, then we could seek the

Lord and pray, but we are in danger of being bombed to death right now."

Park Yong-Ki had a big build, big bright eyes, and an assertive mind. He could be aggressive and blunt, but he was honest. He had come from Manchuria to Pyongyang and then to Seoul and had missed early schooling, so he was two or three years older than his classmates. Now, with his uniform off, he didn't look like a student but more like a mature young adult.

They started up Samgak Mountain, familiar with the terrain. The US forces had already intervened, and sixteen UN member countries had sent contingency forces to fight along with South Koreans, so there was hope that the war would soon be over. But days wasted away without any improvement in the war situation. As their food supply became less, their fear and anxiety grew. And even though they sensed that the Communists were not searching the area, Mang decided to go deeper into the mountain.

"Maybe we should have fled south along with Reverend Bae," questioned Park, obviously irritated.

Mang Eui-Soon was beginning to feel annoyed and ignored his comment. "I think we will be safer here."

Another day passed by. For breakfast, they drank a spoonful of barley mixed with cold water, but by noon they were exhausted. They stopped talking since that exhausted them even more. They tried to breathe slowly and lightly. Park Yong-Ki closed his eyes to block out the blistering sun.

"Hands up!"

Two Communist soldiers, wearing grubby, drab uniforms, along with three young civilians, had surrounded them. They dragged them to the courtyard of an orphanage, prodding their backs and sides with the barrels of their guns as they went. One of them yelled, "You sons of *******, hiding traitors, escaping your homeland, defecting from the People's Liberation Front! We'll beat you pigs to death to save bullets!"

About fifty people were already in the courtyard of Hyangrinwon Orphanage. Most of them were young, stone faced, and stooped over in fear. The Hyangrinwon Orphanage house was empty except for a few blank-eyed little children sitting in one room. Soldiers sat around a table in the middle of the yard. They searched and interrogated people and rummaged through their belongings.

They were divided into two lines. Park Yong-Ki entered the yard; his face was dark, and desperation filled his eyes. When he saw Mang Eui-Soon, he said in a lowered voice, "Please tell them we came here to pray. Tell them this even if they threaten to kill you."

Park Yong-Ki was pulled away by the neck. Mang Eui-Soon closed his eyes and prayed, "Lord, strengthen him, and grant him courage and confidence as your child."

He watched as Park Yong-Ki was interrogated and his packages rummaged through. *No hope is left for us,* he thought. *When Reverend Bae suggested we flee south, I should have listened to him . . . oh, what will happen to us?*

Why are we afraid of death? he thought. *Why have we decided that the bright side is for life and the dark side for death? When we claim ownership of our life, and we think it is taken away, then we are afraid. But are our lives really ours? If our birth was not by our own will, how then can our lives belong to us? Actually, if I am not my own, then why am I worrying?*

When the inquisition of everyone in the line was over, Park Yong-Ki and Mang Eui-Soon were told to leave. "Don't look back! Walk straight ahead! Let's get out of here as fast as we can!" Park Yong-Ki blurted, pulling Mang Eui-Soon.

The six of them, now released, walked hurriedly, hardly daring to breathe. As soon as the orphanage was out of sight, they ran so fast that they almost collapsed in exhaustion. Even though they were quite far away from the orphanage, the echo of gunfire gave their bodies a deathly chill.

Mang halted and gazed up at the sky. "Park Yong-Ki, we are alive, right? We can see sky and earth."

"I don't know why we were spared . . . I found this in my package."

He took out his student ID card from Manturia Teachers' College. "The guy who searched my package asked me how long I was in the school and if I knew a teacher and his nickname," Park Yong-Ki said. "Then he whispered in my ear, 'I graduated from that school, and while I was a student, that teacher—we called him a "white pig"—struck me on the cheeks.' He was so amused, as if one of his long-dead ancestors had appeared to him. Then he told me to promise the interrogator that I would join the volunteer army for the homeland liberation front."

"The Lord has delivered us from death," said Mang Eui-Soon. "It was only possible because of God."

Shots echoed behind him, and the fifty young people in the courtyard were gone. He asked himself, "So why am I joyful?" He suddenly sat down by the roadside. He could not walk anymore. He did not know where he should go or why. Seoul seemed very far away.

The Lord Keeps You

Mang Eui-Soon managed to return home once more to hide under the floor of Hapdong house. Compared to the outdoors it was comfortable enough, and he wished he could stay there. He shuddered at the memory of being pursued in the Chungnung valley and captured on Samgak Mountain.

During Mang Eui-Soon's absence, two students had come to stay at the house: Lee Sung-Soo and Bae Sook-Kyung. Because of the war, the roads to their homes were blocked, and they could not stay in the boarding rooms, so they had sought shelter. Food had run out, however, and Kwonsa La had to carry clothes, utensils, and dishes on her head to exchange for barley or flour in Seoul or beyond. She would lock the house, and, if she could not return that day, the others had to spend the night in the space under the floor with just water. Kwonsa La herself lost a lot of weight and looked like a dried leaf. Her feet had become swollen and sore. She brought in corn, pumpkin, and potatoes—anything that was edible. She walked miles in the summer heat, but still she gave a tearful thanks to God for what she could find.

On the night of July 30, Park visited the Hapdong house. "As Reverend Bae suggested, we should go south by breaking through the frontline. As our troops have retreated further down, we should leave as soon as possible. The longer we delay, the further the frontline is away from us. I am ready to go. My stepmother gave me all her food. At dawn, I will be leaving Seoul."

Elder Mang's house was under constant scrutiny and had been searched several times. Lee Sung-Soo spoke up. "I would like to leave with Park."

"I will follow them," said Bae Sook-Kyung.

Mang Eui-Soon lowered his head. He was afraid to move anywhere. He wanted to stay home. "I will stay with my dad," Mang wanted to say.

"Eui-Soon," Elder Mang called to his son. "I think what Reverend Bae said was right. Leave; the four of you can help each other. God will be with you. God will entrust you with the work you must do."

"But, Dad, I would like to take care of you and stay with you."

"It is God who keeps me," he said, as he raised his bushy eyebrows.

It was a painful night for him as he listened to his father's breathing and thought about leaving him the next day. At dawn, the four of them were ready to slip out of the house separately, promising to meet at the main intersection of Seodaemun gate.

The father charged his son, "I will not worry about you anymore. I believe that God will take care of you. But I have something to say to you. Don't look back. Go forward. Whatever befalls you, do not feel regret. All that happens is necessary for you. Please believe that. Now leave and have a safe trip, my son." His father held him firmly and prayed again. It would be another long, hot day in the middle of July.

Escape to the South

None of the local roads or highways connecting other villages was safe anymore, so they took to the hillsides, staying close to the main roads to keep track of their location. Bombs dropped unpredictably, raining like fire and brimstone from the sky, with a shrieking, ominous sound. Black columns of smoke would billow like a grotesque beast, and the surrounding area became a sea of fire, consuming trees, fields, animals, and people.

Park Yong-Ki sighed, "It is absurd that more than ten UN armies joining the battle cannot expel a single North Korean army and rescue us from this misery!" Mang Eui-Soon appreciated his assertive and open mind. He made the journey more interesting.

They encountered the North Korean People's Army (NKPA) carrying hundreds of recruits in trucks, and the four of them lay flat between the bushes and pines of a lower hillside and watched them. "Oh my goodness, those recruits are just kids!" Park Yong-Ki exclaimed.

"What do those young boys know about pulling triggers? They were forcibly drafted to be disposable bullet shields. Oh God, help them," Bae Sook-Kyung moaned. The long August sun was setting, and the earth, releasing its heat, was suffocating to the exiles.

"We should eat at least one meal of rice a day," said Park Yong-Ki. "If we don't, where will we get enough energy? Please, let's stay here. I will go and find some firewood."

Lee Sung-Soo and Bae Sook-Kyung appreciated Park Yong-Ki's insistence. They took out prewashed dried rice, hot pepper paste, sesame leaf pickles, and cucumber pickles from their knapsacks and looked for a suitable fireplace that wouldn't be noticed while Park Yong-Ki went for the firewood. But when he returned with a water jar but no firewood, his confident look was gone. His feet were dragging, and his eyes and mouth were downcast.

Park Yong-Ki sat down and explained, "I found the owner of a house who had piles of firewood. But what a greedy guy! He wouldn't give or sell me any of it. He said he didn't have enough to get through the winter. He has no idea about tomorrow, the poor creature. With all this bombing, it will become a pile of ashes, anyway. I doubt if he'll live through the winter."

At dawn, they rose and continued their journey. They walked through the barren hillsides, fearful of losing sight of the highways, yet also fearful of coming across them. They had a map, but it was hard to tell which town was which as they went along, and it would be dangerous to ask directions of anyone.

They roughly estimated their location from the position of the sun at that time of the day and from any visible signs on the township offices. Each day, as they continued on, they noticed with sadness the devastated countryside. Rice paddies and fields near the cities were abandoned. Weeds grew everywhere, with corn and millet withered among them. Peppers were crushed to the ground. Farmers' huts were deserted. With the land so ravaged, they wondered how any people left would survive.

In a remote village, they met a farmer working in the fields, removing vines from cucumbers and melons. He gave them several melons the size of a fist. They found a group of bushy pines where they sat down and talked with him.

"We have land and seeds, and therefore, we sow and take care and harvest and share with others. That's so simple," the farmer said. "Why are we engaged in beating, breaking, punishing, and killing each other? By the way, my young friends, why do you venture into such danger?" he asked, creasing his brow.

"We were students in Seoul, but we lost our chance to escape and were stuck there. Now we are returning to our hometowns," they said.

The farmer stared at the sky and said, "I really don't care if I get killed while I am planting or taking care of my crops. A farmer's life is in the fields or paddies. I feel no remorse about dying in a time of war. I live the way I live, and for now, I am alive."

Park Yong-Ki did not join in the conversation. He had taken off his running shoes and was examining his blistered feet. Lee Sung-Soo took off his worn-out leather shoes. The soles of his socks were gone; only the tops and upper parts were left. He ripped the blanket and wrapped the strips around his feet.

"Oh, that smells!" Bae Sook-Kyung said, frowning. "Why don't you take your socks off far away from us?"

"Sis, why are you troubled with this smell? I suggest you have olfactory training in advance. You never know what potent odors are ahead of us," he teased. "Besides, all my toes need a break, and the skin on my heel is all peeled off!"

Day in and day out, they had been covering more than forty kilometers, but now they could walk less and less. They were lucky to have even one meal a day. Whenever they received potatoes from someone, they bowed down many times in appreciation. The weather remained hot and humid.

Park Yong-Ki was dropping farther and farther behind them. The others became so exhausted that they stopped looking back to see where he was, and sometimes he disappeared from view. Everyone had blisters, not only on their feet, but also in their mouths and hearts, and no one uttered a word as they marched.

From Juksan to Geumwang City, they never came across a highway or any local route. When they entered Eumseong City, the terrain around the villages became hilly, and the mountain trails were rough. Bae Sook-Kyung, who had waited for Park Yong-Ki several times, started to grumble half jokingly and half seriously, "Oh my goodness, you have a huge body, but you are a pain. Maybe we will have to leave you behind if you keep slowing us down."

"Sis, I am not pretending. Look, it's like someone has peeled off my skin and sprayed hot pepper on my feet."

"Give me your pack," Mang Eui-Soon said to him, pulling it off his back. Mang Eui-Soon tried an exchange of shoes, but they were too small. Mang Eui-Soon's feet were blistered, too.

"Mr. Mang," said Bae Sook-Kyung, "you didn't say anything about your own feet."

"It's not a big deal. I can still walk. Let's walk, praising God and reciting psalms. That will relieve your pain."

Meanwhile, Lee Sung-Soo and Bae Sook-Kyung were walking along the winding mountain trails far ahead of them. Park Yong-Ki's feet felt as though he was walking over burning charcoal. Carrying Park Yong-Ki's knapsack as well as his own, Mang Eui-Soon's feet didn't feel much better, and beads of sweat flowed down his face. They had no fixed destination, and they felt desolate, as if heaven and earth were against them.

They found a brook and filled their water jars. An old man over seventy was tending a vegetable garden. "Grandpa, where does this mountain trail lead?" asked Lee Sung-Soo.

"Over the hill is Sadamri village," he responded. He was suntanned, dark, and short, and he was confident in thought and speech. "Where are you young people heading for on this trail?"

"We are students in Seoul. We are going back home to our parents, to escape the war. Is the Communist army around here?"

"Do you think that they would miss us on the mountainsides? They swept this poor mountain village, and many sympathizers suddenly turned up. For several days it was quiet while they took our boys and gave them rifles. They either sent them to the front or dragged them away somewhere. My young friends, watch out, because this area is already Red. Good luck."

The old man tucked a handful of green hot peppers and several cucumbers into their bundles and gave them directions to a lone, empty house up ahead.

Park Yong-Ki, who had been dragging his feet like a criminal in shackles, grinned as if he had received a reprieve from death. "Tonight we can sleep under a roof! We can cook that last handful of rice that we have and eat it with cucumbers and green hot peppers!" Suddenly, his walk was energized as he went ahead of them toward the house.

They sat down against the crumbling wall of the deserted house without talking or moving, enjoying the unexpected rest and peace. At that moment, the four forgot completely why they were here and where they were going. They even forgot the feeling of hunger. They were so tired that even if this became their last moment in life, they would die contented.

"Hold it! Don't move!"

Suddenly, men appeared at the door. Rifle barrels were pushed before their eyes. Two Communist soldiers in grubby uniforms and carrying rifles and three young men in civilian clothes carrying bamboo spears and sticks surrounded them. Mang Eui-Soon rose slowly, wondering who had betrayed them.

Lurking Devils

They walked over eight kilometers at gunpoint. Although it was downhill, they were pricked and pushed by the rifle muzzles to hurry along. Suddenly, Park Yong-Ki crumbled to the ground.

"Hey, you son of a *****!" yelled one of the soldiers.

"Shoot him!" yelled the other soldier. Park Yong-Ki could not get up. They kicked him and beat him with their rifles.

Mang Eui-Soon gave one of his bundles to Lee Sung-Soo and the other to Bae Sook-Kyung. Then he turned his back toward Park Yong-Ki.

"Who told you to carry him piggyback, you cheeky son of a *****?"

He kicked Mang Eui-Soon, who fell forward. "Please let me carry him on my back. My friend hurt his feet severely."

The soldiers suddenly became silent for a moment, staring into Mang Eui-Soon's face. "Can you carry him all the way?" a soldier yelled.

"Mr. Mang, I think I can walk now." Park Yong-Ki got up with a sudden vigor and limped along, one step at a time. Mang Eui-Soon held on to him, and they walked together. "Beyond there, is our Lord waiting for us? Is this how we get to be like Jesus?" Park Yong-Ki whispered tearfully.

By the time they got down the mountain road and followed the highway to Goesan, the sun had already set. They were led to a tile-roofed house that had a sign: "People's Committee." It was well known that the People's Committee was made up of convicts from military and civilian prisons. They were thrown into a dark room where the smell almost choked them. Something in the room was moving! People! Silent, suspicious people—their sweat causing the odor.

A subdued voice surfaced above the darkness. "Who are you, newcomers?"

"We are trying to flee the war," replied Lee Sung-Soo. "How long have you been here?"

"It varies. Each day, some have been dragged out and tortured."

At that moment, someone outside screamed at them. "Who's talking in there? You want to get slashed?"

Everyone went quiet. Time stood still. It was all darkness, heat, body odors, and silence.

Then the door was flung open, and a rough voice blurted out, "The woman who just came in, you come out here in a hurry." They meant Bae Sook-Kyung.

Bae Sook-Kyung's screams of distress pierced through the wall. They tried to plug their ears, but her shrieks of terror penetrated to their very bones. Then the door banged open, and the three were called out.

In the bedroom of the tile-roofed house, lit by kerosene lamp, Bae Sook-Kyung sat on a chair, her hands strapped behind her. Her dark blue skirt was ripped, and her thighs exposed. Her legs were cut and bleeding. Her hair was drenched in sweat, which rolled down her face. Her eyes were swelling shut.

"Take off your clothes!"

The three did so, down to their underwear. The flickering light of the lamp revealed their nakedness clearly. "Listen, you fellows," said one of the interrogators. "If you answer honestly, you can live, but if not, you take the consequences." Mang Eui-Soon was questioned first. "You are a retreating South Korean soldier?"

"No, sir."

"You said, 'No'?"

"No, sir."

"Still 'No'?"

He swung at Mang Eui-Soon with his stick, smashing into his waist. "No, sir. No, sir." After several more hits, he fell flat, but he never screamed. He only said, "No, sir," each time he was asked. The two interrogators panted as they lashed him with sticks and punched and kicked him. His nose bled, and his flesh was broken and bleeding profusely.

"Are you out for revenge against us who were freed by the People's Liberation Army?"

"No, sir."

When they got bored with beating him, they began torturing him. They did a leg screw on him. They inserted a stick between the crook of his knees and stepped and trampled on it.

The torture continued by beatings with a stick and a leather whip, then with water being poured into his mouth while he was hanging upside down. When they were finished with him for the moment, they tortured Lee Sung-Soo and Park Yong-Ki in the same way. Mang Eui-Soon, hearing their groans, prayed, "Dear Lord, help them to overcome their pain. Help them not to be defeated. Let them see Jesus climbing the hill of Golgotha. When Jesus was hit with a studded leather whip, his skin was ripped off with each strike. We are suffering this hardship because of our sins, but you suffered because of our sins. Let them remember the words 'He was wounded for our transgressions, he was bruised for our iniquities; upon him was the chastisement that made us whole, and with his stripes we are healed.'"

The interrogator could not bear the idea of Mang Eui-Soon not screaming in pain. So he spat on his hand, held the stick with greater determination, and struck him recklessly on the shoulder, waist, and other parts of the body. In the midst of his flickering consciousness, Mang Eui-Soon was sure that he would die. His body would return to the earth, and his soul would travel to his Lord. It was all beyond his control. The men took turns beating Mang Eui-Soon so that they could each have a break. When day broke, they stopped the beatings and threw the four people into the rear building with the others, who were still sleeping, despite the screaming that had reverberated through the darkness.

"Mr. Mang, are you still listening under these conditions? Are you still listening to God?" Park Yong-Ki asked.

"Even though they smash my body, they cannot crush my spirit. My ears are open more widely."

They learned that the people imprisoned with them, about thirty altogether, were neighbors from the local village who knew each other very well. "Most of those who beat us were not from the North Korean army but our own neighbors who left home to study in the cities and then came home colored in red," said one person. Now they are much more cruel than the NKPA."

At noon, water and a loaf of cooked rice, which was more than half wheat, were shared out. Coarse bits of salt in the rice loaf made it taste like sand.

As night advanced, they called the four out again and seemed to never tire of beating them. "Are you Christians? The Bible, hymnbooks, is that all you know? You will like this better than singing hymns," they said, laughing.

They swung their whips, slashing the empty air in the darkness, and derisively telling them to listen to the songs made by the sweeping strokes. On the fifth day, Lee Sung-Soo and Bae Sook-Kyung were released. Lee Sung-Soo returned to the room and whispered earnestly to Mang Eui-Soon and Park Yong-Ki, "We cannot leave you behind, although we have been told to."

Mang Eui-Soon's face was smashed and swollen, but his eyes were peaceful and tranquil. He replied, "No, don't worry, please, Mr. Lee. Leave here as soon as possible. If we pray fervently for each other, we are together wherever we are. Whatever befalls you, overcome it with faith. The Lord be with you."

Each time it got dark, for ten more long days, the swearing and torture continued. Park Yong-Ki's face was so swollen that he could even not open his eyes. "Mr. Mang, we are becoming pickled vegetables," he smiled feebly. "If we admit what is not true, they will kill us, but if we keep denying it, we will die from the beatings. Mr. Mang, are you going to say as Jesus did on the cross, 'Father, forgive them. They don't know what they are doing'?"

"I have no choice but to keep silent. How far wickedness can drag humans down!"

A few days later, as night fell, a North Korean army officer, accompanied by several soldiers and young men from the People's Committee, rushed in and pulled out the two. That night, the swearing and torture reached a new height. They took out more than half of the imprisoned people. Gunshots reverberated in the darkness, followed by silence.

Mang Eui-Soon blacked out temporarily while he was beaten that night, and when he came to, he heard, "If these ******** are alive after they are beaten, we will let them go, but if not, this place will be their graves." Again he lapsed into unconsciousness. It was the next morning before he regained consciousness. After being beaten and trampled on, they'd been thrown back into the cell.

At sunrise, two soldiers with rifles and a man from the People's Committee ran in. "You two, get up and come with us! Are you listening to us?"

They could not rise. It felt easier to stay where they were and get beaten up. Their faces were slashed and swollen, their broken skin smeared with blood made their clothes stick to their scars, and their hair was like straw.

"Move!" ordered a soldier, thrusting a muzzle at them. Mang Eui-Soon tried to lift his legs, but he couldn't.

"You want to live, don't you? If so, move!"

Mang Eui-Soon thought about the cross on the hill, and slowly, he started to walk. But Park Yong-Ki could not move at all. *Maybe he is paralyzed,* thought Mang Eui-Soon.

A soldier turned his rifle upside down and lashed him on the head with its butt. "Son of a *****, are you making fun of me?" he barked. Park Yong-Ki blacked out.

"Pour water over him," said another soldier.

He slowly regained consciousness, and Mang Eui-Soon put his arms around him to carry him into the room. It was the first time they had seen the room in daylight. Everyone was busy working as if they had never beaten anyone. "Wash yourself first," the man said.

Two basins of water were brought in, and they washed themselves slowly and cautiously, wondering about this sudden twist in their situation. After washing, they were led into a room where they were offered rice and meat-and-potato soup, set on a table in the middle of the floor.

"Sorry for the trouble you have had during the past weeks," the man said. "We, the people of the Liberation Army, who got orders from General Kim Il-Sung to come down to liberate the South, had never beaten or harassed any civilians. Unfortunately, some comrades, showing excessive loyalty to the party, ran into trouble. Forget about what's happened.

Go home, take a few days of rest, and then come and join our army as people's combatants. I will give you certificates for your travel."

They handed them certificates that said these two had taken the people's training courses faithfully during the last twenty days and would become faithful people and go to the war as people's combatants. What a puzzling turnaround! During the last twenty days, these men had inflicted brutal torture on them and tried to make them confess that they had helped the enemy, but now they had suddenly changed their attitude. Why were they being released?

A Long Journey to Canaan

Mang Eui-Soon and Park Yong-Ki rested under the green leaves of an apple tree laden with fresh apples, and between the leaves, they could see the bright sky and the burning sun. What was happening with the war situation? Were slaughter, destruction, and torture still going on? *But here it is serene and comfortable—a kind of paradise,* thought Mang Eui-Soon.

"Mr. Mang, where are we now? And why are we here?" Park Yong-Ki asked with his eyes still closed.

"God has allowed us to taste this bit of paradise, and to meet an angel, in order to give us rest for the next assignment."

There was silence between the two as they relaxed a little longer on the hazy, baked earth under the scorching and incandescent sky.

"You look hungry." They sprang up at the sound of a soft voice. An elegant woman in her mid-forties approached them quietly. Her manner, with its grace and dignity, suggested she was the wife of the farm owner.

"Have some water first, or you will choke," she now said as Mang and Park stood up from under the apple tree. "I don't have a lot to fill your stomachs. If I had saved some chickens, how nice it would have been."

She took them to her house and brought in steamed potatoes and pumpkin pancakes on the trays. As they ate, she cried, telling them about her son, who had gone to the war as an ROKA officer. And she hadn't heard from her husband for ten days, ever since he had been taken to the People's Committee. She was also anxious about her daughter, who attended the university in Seoul and had been there when war had broken out. Only she and the family of her orchard caretaker were left.

They ate so voraciously and hurriedly that they suddenly felt ashamed. She left briefly to bring a bottle of sesame oil and some ginger juice. She proceeded to pour sesame oil on their knees and calves and to spread ginger juice on their wounds.

The wife of the caretaker was stunned when she saw her bringing out the sesame oil. "Madame, you said the sesame oil is the last commodity we have, and it is being saved for your son."

But the woman used it up generously to treat them. "I believe that these two are very special people whom God has helped. It is a miracle that they have no broken bones or internal bleeding." They stayed at the orchard farm for three days, and the wounds and hurts healed almost completely.

Then at dawn, the "angel" saw them off. For three days, she had taken them into her home and cared for them. She felt sadness at their leaving, as if they were her own sons. "I am happy to help you any way I can. Watch out, and keep safe in your future."

The wheat bread they had brought from the orchard was gone in a day, and their hunger now made walking more difficult. And the more severe the hunger became, the heavier their bodies felt. The pass through the mountains still seemed still so far away, while the terrain was getting steeper and rougher. "Mr. Mang, I'm sorry to say this, but I never expected this kind of road. If I had known this, I never would have come."

"A road is a road," answered Mang Eui-Soon. "The road we are walking along is ours. Keep quiet and walk, please."

As they crossed over the third and final crest of the pass, they met a clean-shaven young man dressed in shaggy clothes. It was apparent that he was hiding his status to escape danger. He trusted them in an instant and told them both his status and his name without hesitation. He was Myung Hyung-Churl, the son of a well-known government officer. Now they had another companion.

Hunger and thirst were ever present, a punishment they had to endure. Because of the severe drought, even when they broke off a corn stem, there was no sweet juice to wet their mouths. Army troops had swept through the paddy fields, leaving nothing. Swarms of other refugees had fled over the fields and trampled on them. As they approached the hillside near Nakdong-Myeon District, Park Yong-Ki collapsed beside the road. The sky was burning like a white-hot flame. "Mr.

Mang, please let me stay here. Leave me and just go. I cannot believe there is a Promised Land." Myung Hyung-Churl collapsed beside Park Yong-Ki.

"Look," encouraged Mang Eui-Soon. "There's a town just over there. Maybe there will be some food for us."

They approached the town cautiously, crawling rather than walking. At the town entrance, a feeling of bleak fear compelled them to stop. The town seemed to be abandoned. Where was everyone? Had murderers slaughtered all of the people?

"Maybe they left something to eat in an empty house," Myung Hyung-Churl whispered as he stood up. Along a fence by a house, a sunflower and some myrtle bloomed, like artificial flowers arranged for consoling those who mourn the dead. The town roads were strewn with ripped straw mattresses, straw ropes, broken pieces of ceramic jars, patched quilts, and rags.

"Look, over there!" Myung Hyung-Churl cried as he ran toward a dead horse. He and Park Yong-Ki groped in their bundles for their knives. Fears disappeared. Only a desperate craving for food controlled their bodies and minds. After they had cooked it and had a meal, they took as much of the leftovers as they could carry.

Continuing on, they arrived at Indong-Myeon District, then Sangju City. A river guided them from Sunsan City to Indong City. Before the river became too wide, they crossed it, planning to go down to Daegu City through Waegwan City. But there they encountered a large Communist supply force camped in the barren mountain near an empty town. There were tanks, midrange artillery, trucks carrying ammunition, and even oxcarts.

Finding a public cemetery, they hid against a tomb. They were desperately hungry. It was a long time ago since they had eaten the horse meat; the leftovers had soon spoiled in the heat. Park Yong-Ki said, "I saw an apple farm across the street when we came in here. Shall I go and get some?"

Myung Hyung-Churl was terrified. "The hills are full of Communist troops. Are you crazy?"

"I know, but when it gets dark, I will go."

As the sky darkened, it began to rain. They agreed to go into the orchard together. The instinct for food blinded them to any danger. They would move stealthily and not shake the branches, so no apples would drop onto the ground. They looked around but could see nothing in the dark. The darkness and the rain helped give them cover as they brought back as many apples as they could carry. They bit hungrily into the apples, but they were bitter and not juicy and hard to swallow since they were not ripe yet.

It started to pour heavily, and there was no place to escape the rain. Their sweat-soaked clothes became drenched and let off a stuffy, fishy odor, and the soaking rain chilled them. Mang Eui-Soon tipped his head, collecting raindrops in his mouth, and answered, "Today is September 3, and Sunday." He was counting the days so that he would not forget the Lord's Day. "And for the sacrament, we are served apples and rain," he added.

Park Yong-Ki sighed as if he could not bear anymore. "Let's go down to the town. Maybe the soldiers have moved toward the frontline. If we stay here, this chilly rain will penetrate into our bones and empty stomachs, and the three of us will drown in this graveyard. I think the town might be empty now, and if we can get dry, we might live. Also, we have certificates from the Honorable People's Combatants, saying we have completed twenty days of training and will become faithful people's combatants when we return to our hometown."

It was raining so heavily that they could not easily see where they were going. When they reached the town, all was quiet. They entered a thatched house that had its doors open. In the kitchen, they found some firewood and some matches. When they reached under the firewood, they uncovered a few jars of glutinous rice and sesame seeds. They added the glutinous rice and sesame seeds to a kettle, poured in water, and set the fire. They were able to dry their clothes and personal belongings before the fire. While the others were busy cooking and drying wet clothes, Mang Eui-Soon sat despondently.

"Mr. Mang, is anything wrong?" asked Park Yong-Ki.

"When the owners of this house come back and find these jars, they will be greatly disappointed!" Mang Eui-Soon answered. "I can just imagine their expressions and feelings. We are getting along by stealing from others."

"Mr. Mang, you are too sentimental! We are stuck in a terrible war, and life vanishes like leaves falling from trees. All that is ours has been taken away, and here you are, worried about a few handfuls of rice. I have an idea. Write on a piece of paper that we were so hungry, we took food. After this war, we will repay what we have taken. We can leave our names and addresses."

"Wow," he said, "the smell of that rice cooking is making me crazy! I've never known such a wonderful smell!" The three young men ate the rice voraciously, making sure they grabbed every last grain of rice. Their stomachs were full, and their wet clothes had dried. The sound of the rain on the roof made everything cozy, and soon they lay flat on the warm floor in a deep sleep.

"Get up, you stupid sons of *******, or I'll shoot you!"

The muzzles of the guns of five Communist soldiers surrounding them prodded them in the ribs several times to wake them up.

The three, now fully awake, put their hands on their heads as they were searched. It was dawn, and the rain had stopped. *What price will we pay for eating a scanty bit of rice and having a sound sleep under a roof?* wondered Mang Eui-Soon.

"Where are you coming from?" asked one of them, as two young civilians joined the soldiers.

Park Yong-Ki explained the situation as convincingly as he could. "Here are our certificates. We missed the chance for joining the People's Combatants. Our hometown is Jinju City, and when we arrive there, we are prepared to devote ourselves to the People's Liberation. Look at this, sir."

It was apparent that these people were in a hurry to flee from something, because the soldier took a quick glance at the certificate and then hurriedly left. They were free!

It was still early morning, but the sky was clear. Across the village street, they saw advancing diesel tanks, which shrieked along, the noise almost piercing their eardrums. Some tanks were carrying big, beaklike cannons, kicking back the muddy clay, wet from last night's rain, as they went. The short, stark howitzers were uncovered, and the trucks carrying the mid-range cannons were terrifying.

Leaving the village, they entered the barren mountains, but someone followed them. Their hearts jumped. Would they be detained again? It was one of the civilians who had been with the soldiers.

The civilian saw their fear and rushed to speak, "You should tear up the certificates. People carrying these papers are deemed suspicious and are at anyone's disposal. The soldiers had been at the front and did not know about the certificates. I ran after you to inform you and am almost out of breath. Please believe me and destroy them. Heaven helped you. Near Waegwan City, there is a fierce battle across the Nakdong River. Take care." Then he ran back down to the village.

"Oh my goodness, we carried our own death sentences!" cried Park Yong-Ki, tearing up the certificate he had so cherished. Passing the area where the battle scene was still fresh, they saw the destroyed army tanks of the North Koreans and a dead Communist soldier in his mustard-colored uniform, smeared with blood, fallen beside a smashed mortar. A bombed tent appeared to have been the field headquarters. They were confused about where to go. Evidently the frontline was not far away. But how could they reach the South Korean army? How could they break through the enemy line?

Again they were captured. This time they were taken to a place where the Communist army and civilians were working on military supplies. Their examination was not a rigorous one, and it seemed that helping hands were needed so badly that whether they were enemies or strangers didn't matter. They were put to work. The three young men were allocated to the kitchen, where they washed and cooked a pile of rice as high as a mountain.

It wasn't all bad, for there was a brook and woods nearby, and they had food to eat. Sometimes when the cooked rice was too hard, they pounded it with salt in a mortar in order to make rice loaves.

They heard the enemy soldiers discussing the war when they came to eat the rice, and Park Yong-Ki, pounding a pestle, whispered to Mang Eui-Soon, "There's going to be an end to all this soon."

Mang Eui-Soon smiled and continued to make loaves earnestly. The hot summer weather had changed, and once the rain started, it continued. A tent was put up where the loaves were made, but rain splashed in and it became cold. Each time his hands pressed rice into a loaf, he nodded as if he were bowing. The graceful silhouette of Mang seemed carved in the light from an electric bulb. "Are you sleepy? Or are you beating the rhythm to lighten the load?" Park Yong-Ki asked him, pounding a mortar. Mang Eui-Soon was quiet awhile and replied in a whisper, "I am praying."

"Whom are you praying to? To this loaf?"

"I pray to God to preserve those who eat these loaves and to let them realize the wickedness and vanity of the war and be awakened to love."

Park Yong-Ki thought this was sad and futile. He felt enraged instead. He threw a handful of sand into the rice when he bent to pound the mortar. He wanted to hit Mang hard, but instead he pounded the mortar harder. Suddenly, he felt that all their miseries were caused by the ineptitude of Mang Eui-Soon.

As the frontline moved, so did the kitchen, often in the middle of the night. But the cooking job did not continue. The three young men were next made to carry cannonballs in the dark of night along the riverside. When it occurred to him that cannonballs kill many people when they explode, Mang Eui-Soon stopped a moment.

He was hit on the back by a rifle butt. "Why are you so slow? Work faithfully and see the completion of the war! You reactionary *******, don't you try to run!"

His shoulder, protected only by a thin summer shirt, could not withstand the hit, and he stumbled. He was cut and bruised. Park Yong-Ki and Myung Hyung-Churl approached him and whispered, "Don't get too far from us. Even if they hit you, stay close to us. Since it's dark, it will be easy to avoid being seen. When we find a chance, we will escape."

After midnight, a signal flare illuminated the darkness, and bombing followed. Park Yong-Ki and Myung Hyung-Churl took advantage of the chaos to take Mang Eui-Soon and crawl out of the place. "The Communist frontline is in disarray," said Park Yong-Ki confidently.

"The frontline is somewhere around here, and if we can cross it, then we will be all right," Myung Hyung-Churl responded.

"We are worthy to be called experienced warriors," boasted Park Yong-Ki. "We have two day's worth of food because when the ******** gave out the loaves, I tricked them and saved some extra for us."

The next morning when they bit the loaves, they couldn't chew any of them. They were full of sand.

The Curse of Misunderstanding

The fierce and decisive battle continued. The Communists, who had taken all of South Korea except Daegu and Busan, were pushing to engulf whatever remained. Meanwhile, the Korean and UN armies were desperate to push them back and recapture the land, using the last two cities as springboards.

The three friends advanced during lulls of artillery fire, but otherwise, they hid themselves and waited. Airplanes ceaselessly shook the sky and thrashed the ground with bombs. After each bombing, machine-gun fire followed. The air was cloudy because of gunpowder smoke, and the ground was dug up and turned over, so they could not discern their direction.

It was early morning when they came to a town by a bridge spanning a river near Waegwan City. On the street, things were strewn everywhere, indicating pandemonium: rice, quilts, gourd bowls, spoons, pans, and shoes sat like orphans, evidence that refugees must have very recently fled the area.

They swept some rice into a bag, planning to cook it later. On the road along the riverbank, smashed motorbikes, apparently belonging to Communist troops, were lying about, and bleeding bodies were spread out like laundry on the boulders.

They dashed by, covering their mouths and noses with their hands.

Finding no place and no time to hide, they kept on running. Arriving at a village in flames, they saw no troops, neither enemy nor friend, although they sensed it was a place where their own troops had been stationed. A pile of ration boxes sizzled in the fire, and stray oxen and pigs rushed about frantically.

They were amazed to find some rice boiling in a kettle, in the middle of courtyard, over a fire. “Oh, what nice people! They’ve cooked rice for us,” exclaimed Park Yong-Ki.

Myung Hyung-Churl dashed to the kettle. “This is really a gift from God, who has favored Mr. Mang for his good conduct.”

But turning his back on them, Mang Eui-Soon stood with his head bowed.

“Why are you standing there? Our troops seem to have abandoned this place only recently. We should hurry to catch up with them.”

In a nearby trench lay the dead body of a boy about six years of age. His eyes were closed and his face clean. The blood seeping from his stomach was still warm.

“Let’s bury him.”

“No, it’s too dangerous. The enemy could show up at any moment.”

Park Yong-Ki and Myung Hyung-Churl were angry. The midday sun was burning hot, and the pungent smell and heat coming from the burning buildings and flames choked them.

"Then you go first, and I will follow you," said Mang Eui-Soon. "I'll meet you at the corner of the mountainside." And he left, entering an empty house to find a shovel. The two could not leave him, however, so they anxiously waited for him. He came out with the shovel and dug the ground beside the furrow.

"That's good enough. Bury him," Park Yong-Ki urged impatiently. Mang Eui-Soon quietly continued digging. The ground was soon deep enough to cover the dead boy. Park Yong-Ki and Myung Hyung-Churl lifted the boy and gave him to Mang Eui-Soon, who embraced him in his arms and closed eyes.

"Lord, you took this little life in the midst of all this misery and saved him and received his soul. I believe you took his soul to give him rest." The two took him and placed him in the earth and hurriedly shoveled in the dirt.

The next afternoon, they found another abandoned village, lying naked under the early autumn sun. The desolate village had been stripped and plundered. They entered it very cautiously and fearfully, but they met no one. Park, who had walked a bit ahead of them, shouted, "Look, it's the South Korean flag!"

"We broke through the frontline! We are over it! This is our land for sure!" exclaimed Myung Hyung-Churl, jumping into the air.

"Then where are they now?" asked Mang Eui-Soon. "Why is no one here? We'd better look around and check on the situation rather than moving on recklessly."

Suddenly, a door was flung open, and two rifle muzzles were pointed at them. “Hands up!” said two Americans in English.

Mang Eui-Soon stepped forward and calmly explained in English that they were civilian refugees. The Americans seemed curious and amused with Mang Eui-Soon because of the way he spoke English. They talked through their wireless transmitter while Mang Eui-Soon answered their questions, calmly and simply. Then a US military jeep drove up to take them to the camp.

“What a relief! Maybe they will take us in a car in appreciation of our toil and sweat. We are war veterans,” said a grinning, rejuvenated Park Yong-Ki. Behind them, flames rose up from the mountains. The three young men breathed a sigh of relief. If the Americans had not found them, they might have ended up as a handful of ash.

“God has delivered us from hellfire,” exclaimed Park Yong-Ki.

“The Americans are angels sent by God!” Myung Hyung-Churl cried. “They are God’s messengers to deliver us from hell. I am sure that the God of Mang and Park is the God of love.”

“Yes, and he is your God, too. He is pleased with your confession,” said Mang Eui-Soon, looking back over the sea of fire. Then he whispered, “But there is a reason we have survived and a reason for the hellfire. Once we understand the reasons, we will have a mission to do something about it.”

A second-generation Japanese-American sergeant was sent to them as an examiner. Although he was also Asian, he treated the three as if they were another race. He looked with suspicion at Mang Eui-Soon, who spoke in English and Japanese as he described their history in detail. "We are students from Seoul. We were captured, tortured, recaptured, imprisoned, and made to do compulsory labor. We have brought a Bible and a hymnbook."

The examiner was as cold as steel as he threw a barrage of questions at them about the routes the three had taken. "We have actually captured many Communist spies who were carrying Bibles," he said. "You don't have any identification. And we know how spies can fabricate identification."

Several other officers came in. They listened to what he explained to them and then signed some papers. *What was there on the signed paper?* the three wondered as they watched the examiner's eyes. Soldiers came in a jeep, and the sergeant showed them the papers and spoke to them briefly, saying that the fate of the three would be determined in Daegu.

"What is going on here?" yelled an outraged Park Yong-Ki. "How can they treat us like this? Maybe they cannot award us the prizes we deserve, but still, what are they doing to us? Do they really think we are Communist spies?"

"Let's calm down," said Mang Eui-Soon. "Remember, we are at the frontline. When we get to Daegu, we can talk to the people in Korean, and they will understand us. They will be different from the foreigners. It's no use to protest here, so let's leave quietly."

As they rode along in the jeep, they watched as villages and riversides, sky and earth, all became a sea of fire. It was after sunset when they arrived at the Daegu police station.

People were shouting, screaming, and running up and down, and babies were crying. They were taken inside, and their papers were thrown down on a desk, and the jeep left in a cloud of dust.

"Where are you coming from?" a man asked them gently.

"From Waegwan," answered Mang Eui-Soon. "We met the US soldiers, who examined us and sent us here."

"Then you are prisoners of war. The United States considers anyone caught within two miles of the front, refugees or not, as war prisoners."

"Are you sure?" Park Yong-Ki and Myung Hyung-Churl laughed.

But by morning, they realized how serious the situation was. It seemed everyone was suspect. They saw women, children, old people, and even a whole family among those imprisoned. Later, the mothers, grandmothers, and children were released, but not the men. "How can you treat us like this? We have clear identification. Let us go!" But their protests were coldly ignored.

They implored a policeman who came with a ration of a rice loaf, but he bluntly said he knew nothing about it. In the afternoon, they were called out. Maybe now they could get a review of their case! But it was a three-quarter-ton army truck that awaited them.

"Where are you taking us?" Mang Eui-Soon asked an armed soldier who carried bundles of documents.

"To Busan."

"Why should we go to Busan?" he inquired. "We are civilian refugees from Seoul, students. Why don't you review our cases here? Why are we under surveillance and suspicion?"

"You talk too much," the frenzied soldier yelled. But Mang Eui-Soon continued: "Why waste manpower in this time of war? We are truly students. You can handle our case here. Please present our case to those who could make a decision. We are students who have suffered so much hardship to come to our fatherland."

"Shut up with your nonsense. You are compulsory laborers for the Communists, or you are spies. This paper proves it. Get on the truck!"

At that moment, Park Yong-Ki roared like a fierce beast. "Why on earth don't you believe us? What's the use of that paper? Americans made that all up. We are Koreans. We are students who love this country. What can such a stupid paper tell about us?"

The soldier smashed Park Yong-Ki in the back with the butt of his rifle. "Get on the truck," he said, pointing his rifle at him.

They arrived at the Daegu railroad station, where several black cargo cars were waiting. There were many other people about to be loaded onto the train. Ranks were formed and the numbers counted. When the doors of the cargo cars were opened, they were pushed and pulled and beaten by clubs to get aboard without the help of a ramp. Inside the ramshackle car, Communist soldiers in tattered, drab uniforms were strewn about like rags, looking out the door with blank expressions on their faces. Heaps of trash lay in the corner. The pungency of excrement filled their nostrils.

Park Yong-Ki yelled to one of the two guards, "Why are you taking us along with Communist prisoners? This should not happen!"

"You *******, shut up," the guard yelled back.

"Oh, kill me now!" Park Yong-Ki wailed like a wounded beast. "Is this the gift I receive from my country, my fatherland?"

From somewhere in the dark, someone hurled piercing words at him in the North Korean dialect. "You son of a *****. You dirty pig, betraying your comrades. When you're captured, you're captured. What are you crying for? Do you deny you are from the People's Army? If you are not NKPA, then get the **** out of here. We don't want to be considered the same as you. Just get the **** out."

Myung Hyung-Churl slumped down and buried his face in his hands, while Mang Eui-Soon held on to the frenzied Park Yong-Ki. He closed his eyes and prayed quietly, "We have no place to stand. We have nowhere to go. Lord, what is this for? Lord, help us to be resolute. Hold us fast. I know that this is just part of what we have to go through. Help us to listen humbly to you and to wait silently on you."

Then he whispered to Park Yong-Ki, "When we get to Busan, we will prove ourselves students. Don't get discouraged. War is like that. Everyone is in a panic. Be patient and wait in silence. The way will open up to us. Actually, those who are captured here are more desperate. We should comfort them and pray for them. If we are rowdy here, they might harm us. Don't annoy them. Act with discretion. Our country suspects us and threw us in here beside people who consider us their enemy."

Park Yong-Ki sobbed, "It's all right. I'll be quiet. I'll endure the suffering and pray ceaselessly. Then we will get what we deserve."

"Any prize we get will be from heaven," said Mang Eui-Soon as the door of the freight train slammed shut and all went dark. The stench was overpowering.

198 [illegible]24 34 202

「十字架의 道」

「本文」『十字架의 道가 滅亡하는 者에게는 미련한 것이요, 救援을 얻는 우리에게는 하나님의 能力이라. (고전 1:18)』

『유대人은 표적을 求하고 헬라人은 智慧를 求하나, 우리는 十字架에 못박히신 그리스도를 傳하니 유대人에게는 거리끼는 것이오 異邦人에게는 미련한 것이로되 오직 부르심을 입은 者들에게는 유대人이나 헬라人이나, 그리스도는 하나님의 能力이오 하나님의 智慧니라』(고전 1:22-24)

1. 유대人은 거리끼는 것이라.

「옳도다, 저희는 믿지 아니함으로 꺾기우고, 너는 믿음으로 섰느니라」(로 11:20)
「罪人으로서 어떻게 이러한 異蹟을 行하겠느냐?」(요 9:16)
義人에게야 異蹟을 行할 技能이 있다. 価値顛倒.

2. 헬라人에게는 미련한 것.

A. 헬라人들은 神은 人사랑할수 없다. 慾求의 사랑
아가페의 사랑은 [illegible]을 주는 사랑, 本能的으로 용서 할려는 神의 [illegible]다」

B. 神과 人이 서로 交通할수 없는 것은 自明의 理다. → 成肉身은 神의 타락이다.
神들은 破滅과 變化 있는 人生存在에서 멀리 뚝 떨어져 祝福과 죽엄 없는 永遠한 생명을 즐기고 있다. Plato 神은 人과 사귈 必要가 없다.

C. 神은 智者를 사랑 (사랑 한다면) 한다.

十字架의 道는

a) 罪人을 부르시고 容赦하시는 하나님의 사랑의 表現입니다.
유대人은 義人을 사랑한다고 생각하고, 헬라人들은 하나님은 사랑을 할수가 없다고 하나. 헬라人은, 神이 萬一 사랑하신다면 智者를 사랑하신다고 생각하였으나 하나님은 미련한 者들을 택하사 지혜 있다고 자랑하는 傲慢한 人生들을 부끄럽게 하였다.

b) 交通할수 없는 神이 아니다. 人類歷史의 한복판에 나타나신 具体的인 神이요, 神의 타락이 아니고 神의 成肉身이오, 우리가 그의 榮光을 보매, 하나님의 獨生者의 榮光이오 恩惠와 眞理가 充滿하였다.

PART THREE
My Cup Overflows

Chang Hyung-Jin:
The Story of Our Friendship Continues

POW

In March 1951 in Busan I heard about his imprisonment in a war camp. It was just a few days after I had returned to Busan from Cheju Island, where I had fled. The news came to me immediately as if it had been waiting for me. On that day the dusty winds of March powdered the city and the sea and unearthed debris, throwing everything around, and seemed to blurt out the news about this man who might end up suffocated under the weight of the tyranny of history.

No visitors. After exploring every avenue to reach him, I was able, at last, to contact Captain Yu Chung-In, who was working at the Third Army Hospital in Busan. She became the bridge between Mang Eui-Soon and me. Although she took advantage of her status as an active army captain, it was not that easy for her to contact him in person. She had to find someone else who would be able to exchange books and letters with Mang Eui-Soon. Sometime in April, Captain Yu Chung-In sent me a bundle of Mang Eui-Soon's letters, along with a brief note and her office address through another person.

Hoping that someday I would receive his letters, he had written to me in his neat hand, one paragraph following another. Pencil and paper were so scarce that he had written on the backs of charts or on the rough paper used for packages, which he would then glue together. His letters came to me like miraculous butterflies, against all odds, and I found I could not read them at first. I wept in despair.

Forced Confession

SEPTEMBER 1950

Dear Hyung-Jin,

I wonder how different it is to be alive or to be dead. Is it true that to be alive is light, and to be dead is dark, and to live is joy, and to die is sorrow? Are you alive, and if you are, what are you doing? My longing for you and my anxiety about you have made a deep furrow in my heart. But that feeling of yearning and anxiousness arises because I am alive. You may wonder what I had to go through to secure paper and pencil to write. I have realized through all this difficulty that life is limited in means, and death is the one way to freedom. You, my friend, live in my heart, whether you are in this world or in heaven. You mean a great deal to me, more than I can say.

I am a prisoner of war. I became a prisoner of war although I have neither grabbed a rifle nor confronted anyone as an enemy. They stamped POW on my clothes, so whatever I wear, I am indelibly branded as a prisoner of war, which for me means a criminal of war. I have become one of the throngs of stigmatized POWs, and I watch them helplessly with sadness. I ask myself how many of them really wanted to take up rifles.

I feel calm—some might think this a defiant attitude—about the unfair treatment I have received. I firmly believe that I am not a war criminal. I am innocent. But I ask myself, am I innocent of all that was happening around me? Did I contain any seeds of war in myself, such as greed, wickedness, jealousy, arrogance, boasting, justification, and self-centeredness? If I cannot stand my ground without a pang of conscience before those questions, I cannot truthfully declare that I did not make any contribution to the outbreak of war.

I decided to resign myself to being a prisoner, that I would confess to being a war convict and live with that. As I accepted this, all the things that have happened to me suddenly merged together as precious, beautiful, and purifying. When I came to this understanding, my eyes were clearly opened to the immense grace bestowed on me. I am looking at you now with a new insight. It's a miracle that I have a friend. That miracle has transformed me, unlocked my soul, and opened up my heart like a budding flower. This is like starlight in a place of darkness. I write to you believing that once we were in the grip of fear and anxiety, but now we are united, and you are listening to me, and I am listening to you.

People call this place Kojeri. It's a name that alludes to waterside embankments, but we cannot see the sea nearby.

If there were embankments, the sea would be near, and we would smell ocean breezes and hear the sound of waves, but that is just a wishful dream.

In place of ocean waves, we have waves of tents that fill the field. Hundreds or maybe thousands of green US Army tents are being set up in the field. When we arrived here, we heard that the US Army had launched the Inchon landing operation. At this news, we instantly shouted "Bravo," but then we found ourselves prisoners, captured by our own army, prisoners of South Korea. When we were unloaded from the freight train at the Busan Railroad Station and transported to this place, we felt consumed by the unfairness of it. We longed for our refugee claimant status to be reviewed. We believed that once our cases were reviewed, we would be declared innocent from these false accusations and set free.

This place was a model of hell—pandemonium, a demonic battlefield, with multitudes of bloodstained, wounded Communists, soldiers in ragged uniforms, prisoners with dirty faces, all indistinguishable from one another in shared misery. They were the North Korean Communist Army, Chinese soldiers, and civilians. The authorities in the Korean and US armies were quite at a loss as to how to deal with them. The intelligence agent of the US Army was in charge of the claimant review, and he worked with an interpreter. The three of us—Park Yong-Ki, Myung Hyung-Churl, and me—were to be processed at the same time.

When they heard our account of why we were carrying the ammunition and rice loaves before meeting up with the US Army, the examiner and interpreter appeared to be relieved. When we were asked to repeat that statement, we described the scene more vividly and passionately because we thought this might bring a favorable decision to us.

"That was complicity with the enemy. That was against the national interest. You gave benefit to the enemy." The interpreter's eyes grew large, and he stared at the three of us.

"How can you call that an act of complicity with the enemy?" said Park Yong-Ki. "We were taken by force and pushed at gunpoint and coerced to work to save our lives. If you were in that situation, do you think you could disobey such a command?"

The interpreter appeared older than us by only one or two years. He had a strong physique and was a handsome young man. He looked very serious, but could he appreciate the course of action we had taken? He frowned in disapproval and said in an intimidating voice, "Listen, you idiots. Who do you think was the target of the ammunition you were carrying on your blistered backs? And what about the Communist ******* who ate the rice loaves that you supplied? Who were they firing their guns at? Who did they try to kill?" He blatantly considered us to be nothing but scum. The review court would determine whether we lived or died. Park Yong-Ki could not remain quiet. He alternated between rage and pleading, stressing that he was a student.

Our review continued the following afternoon. It was not actually continued, but postponed, as if they were tired of our case. They called us in, and then pushed us back, and then called us in again as if they had suddenly remembered us. This was repeated several times. Finally, the interpreter tried to persuade us. "Sign here, and you can enjoy a comfortable life."

He slid the document across the desk, and I examined it thoroughly. It had been issued by the US Eighth Army and claimed that we were spies for North Korea. I said, "No, this is not true. We cannot sign that. We are not afraid to die, but we cannot admit to these terrible acts. We won't sign this."

The interpreter was annoyed and seemingly resolute in coercing us to sign. I realized why he was so desperate. He did not want to risk releasing us until our identity had been cleared. It was easier for him to imprison us. We realized that this was not the court to discern black from white through reasoning and logic. Our quantity and quality of truth did not matter, and we could not avoid the outcome in front of us. They returned my hymnbook and Bible to me without saying anything and gave us clothes emblazoned with the letters *POW*.

In love,
Mang Eui-Soon

October 1950

Dear Friend,

I heard that Seoul was recaptured. Where and how did you struggle in the war? When we meet, we can take our time talking things over, as there are a multitude of untold stories in the letters. I am assigned to the fourth camp, and both Park Yong-Ki and Myung Hyung-Churl are in the fifth camp, right next to mine, so we have a chance to meet from time to time. These camps are apparently designated as prisoner wards to receive wounded soldiers and general patients. Most of the patients are in very serious condition.

After being moved to the fourth camp, I was selected as a hospital aide. The nurses are mostly from the US Army and need interpreters. Since I speak simple English, they frequently look to me to interpret, and I assist in filling out the medical charts.

Dear friend, how can I describe all that I am going through every day? We often emphasize the stress of mental suffering more than the physical, and inevitably we reach the conclusion that physical pain can be endured more easily than mental suffering. But how can I express the suffering and the agony that exist in the mutilated and smashed bodies of these patients? Here, they classify as "light" the cases of gunshot wounds or shrapnel embedded in the body. It is agony to hear the cries of patients who have had their limbs amputated or who have lost their eyesight.

I cry for the sad faces around me. Is there any other real existence than pain? Pain is a definitive driving force by which we realize the existence of our humanity and by which we carve out that existence clearly. What do they have to look forward to? They can only return to the confinement of this camp after having their limbs amputated or losing their eyesight.

A soldier whose two arms had been amputated shouted in rage, with wide eyes and a foaming mouth, "You sons of dead pigs! Come out, I'll kill you! Give me back my arms, my arms! I have to go back to my hometown, and I have to work on my farm!" Yelling frantically he wept and pleaded, "I have old parents and a simple, hardworking wife and two children. If I don't work, they will starve to death. Get my hands back. Get them back!"

For whom did they give their arms? For whom did they give their legs? They are not so much prisoners of war as prisoners of pain, prisoners of fear, sorrow, and loneliness. This is a hellish place, full of suffering. There are so many wounded soldiers as well as patients with internal health problems. In addition to external wounds, many suffer from inflammation and suppuration. Innumerable patients suffer from tuberculosis and liver and gastrointestinal diseases. The US surgeons were shocked by the discovery of so many parasites inside the gastrointestinal tracts. To them these patients seemed dirtier than animals and like such a nuisance.

It is too much to expect compassion from them. I understand that Americans are not solely to blame for their insensitivity. I don't think they are inhumane so much as overwhelmed with the enormous number of patients swarming into the clinic and the severity of chronic diseases, untreated for so long. Compared to the number of incoming patients, doctors are in very short supply. The schedule of the medical team seeing the new patients was so tight that the doctors were not available for the bedridden patients who anxiously waited for them.

"Why can't these people wait their turn?" grumbled a meticulously clean and handsome US surgeon, a major, disapprovingly. "Even if they miss their turn, we cannot do much about it. The patients in this tent are not the war-wounded. They had illnesses before the war and came here with them. We are providing them with a special favor, so why can't they just calmly wait in line?"

I almost choked on this gross insult. Why do these surgeons so arrogantly put down these patients? I wept as I struggled to move the poor patients back to their beds to wait their turn.

To be continued . . .

My Dear Friend,

When the daily routine is over, I am supposed to return to my assigned place, but I like to stay with the patients to attend to them. But that is against the rules, so I soon have to return to my tent.

Inside the tent, there are only straw mats. Clutching their small bundles, the prisoners sleep, curling themselves up to protect their belongings. The United States is a rich country, but of what use are its riches? They are embarrassed by the war; therefore, they are having difficulty being compassionate to the prisoners of war.

There is no light in any of the prisoners' tents, and batteries are supplied only to the guards at the entrance to the tent city. People confined inside the tents rather enjoy the darkness, I think, and are able to release their thoughts and emotions, confined for so long, through fancy pictures of imagination. When they fall asleep, I kneel down on the mat, as I have a healthy body in the midst of the suffering and agony. I pray for those who have lost limbs or eyes, who groan in pain from their infestations, or who cry miserably because they were not allowed to die. In this valley of suffering, a prisoner prays for the prisoners.

Yet sometimes I feel lost and cannot clearly understand what I should seek. With my body intact and healthy, how am I able to perceive their pain and agony and pray for them? How can I seek help for those who are sunk in a fathomless despair, who have accepted their hopelessness as an eternal punishment? My prayers seem to be powerless. Should I pray for their health and strength to be restored, or for their life to end immediately so their suffering could be taken away?

In these moments, I am always too distressed to interpret the love of God in relationship to these people who have survived so many perils and so much death, only to be slashed, ripped, infested, and covered with blood and pus. I've lost the faith that God is love—and lost my will to understand the meaning of it all. I cannot understand the meaning of carnage and the war that caused bodies to be mutilated and lives crushed.

My dear friend, where are you, and what are you doing now? I miss you. Our country that we shared together has been abandoned to ruin. Our hearts have been devastated by hatred and grievances, and they have become barren with mistrust. From the depths of my exhausted soul, I cry to God. And I call to you, my friend, in a soft voice.

With love to you,
Mang Eui-Soon

Life behind Barbed-Wire Fences

October 1950

My Dear Friend,

Two layers of barbed wire surround our prison camp. The dimensions of this confined area are unknown to me, but I can see that the barbed wire is wrapped around firmly planted concrete posts. Inside this barbed-wire fence a new human community has been created. Prisoners sometimes go outside the camp to work, unloading military supplies at the piers, building embankments, or cutting trenches at the foothills of the mountains near Busan. Ironically, some prisoners have had to set up the barbed wire under the careful watch of the guards, thus reinforcing their own confinement.

The expanse of blue sky and the continuous mass of earth were always there, but the two layers of barbed wire that surround our camp create a stark separation between the outside world and us. Every day, new POWs arrive; the number of prisoners is increasing enormously. It makes me think that if the North Korean government mobilized this number of troops, the war should have ended by now. People coming to this place are, without exception, initially perplexed. They shake their heads left and right in fright, but they soon adapt to the grim environment and look forward to any opportunity for work outside the camp.

The sky was blue yesterday, is blue today, and will be blue tomorrow. A camp entrance looks across the Koje stream and the plain of reeds and paddy field. The mosquitoes harassed us for a while when we arrived here.

I assume that this place used to be a swamp and lowlands, as far off I see fluffy white reeds fluttering in the wind.

I heard Seoul had been recaptured and our troops were advancing northward, but I wonder how and where and under what conditions this war might end. I believe that God created each one of us according to his will, but we painted this small country with layers of blood, and before that blood was dry, blood of foreigners was also poured out. I don't know how God will use this country in the future.

It feels like fall now, as the color of the sky has changed. I am going to send you my heart along with songs of autumn. Please take them.

Yours sincerely,
Mang Eui-Soon

NOVEMBER 1950

Dear Friend,

The persimmon trees growing on the foothill of Chungmyo Mountain here have started to change to their fall colors, and I can imagine the ripening fruit on them. The mountains, now draped in their dark, drab, and lifeless winter clothes, are depressing. I am in a stalemate; I can't pray properly. Fall has made my soul miserable and desolate. In the daytime, I am overwhelmed with the immensity of the patients' pain, a suffering that simmers like boiling water. But in the night, I pray, "Why? Why? Why?" and I feel abandoned. My lips freeze, and songs of praise dry up in my mouth. Hymns, which used to soften and unlock my soul, have become cold. I cannot find the melodies, and the words feel strange to me.

You will remember how hymns were always a comfort and strength to me, how they renewed my life. How often we sang those hymns to God, who took away my burden of sins, gave a true peace, gave a true comfort, and hid my soul in the cleft of the rock!

Now my soul is naked, wandering, without shelter, cold and alone. It's not because I became a POW, nor is it because I am being watched and confined by two layers of barbed-wire fence, but rather because of the great despair of the people here in the prison camp that I am in such a state.

The number of ailing people is staggering. Patients, desperately waiting for doctors and medicine, battle each other to be the first in line to get help. And they have needs not only for food, daily supplies, medicine, and doctors' attention, but something else. I know them. Their bodies are brutalized, and their souls are naked, deprived, deserted, and shrunken. I know what I should offer to them, but I agonize over my inability to bring them comfort. When I kneel to pray, I feel helpless. In trying to pray, I become despondent and overwhelmed at the immensity of it all. How can my solitary prayer alleviate the depth of the tragedy? Inside this barbed wire, there is no room to accommodate anyone's uniqueness of personality, character, career, education, or family genealogy. All human attributes are completely absent. People are reduced to their basic survival instincts, fighting against friends or neighbors for a spoonful of soup or a grain of rice. I feel I have no definitive answer to offer them, and even if I did, would they be receptive to it?

One time as I knelt in the dark, a stranger approached me from where he'd been hiding in a corner. He said, "It's wrong, wrong! The God who loved you absolutely and whom you love, loves blood. If he is the creator of everything, then he also created war and made the hearts and hands of those who kill humans as if they were killing flies. He wants to taste blood continuously. Does he now give you peace? He let his Son get nailed on the cross to save you. The cross of Golgotha redeemed sin. So if his love is so complete, why is there still slaughter on this earth? Do you still think God is love when he gives birth only to rip his children apart and open the gates of hell for them? They die screaming! It's all wrong, wrong. Furthermore, your prayers are useless to help anyone. So stop doing it. It's ridiculous. God has turned his back on you completely. Do you really think you can move God with your prayers in this situation? Never!"

As this continued, I became afraid. I decided not to accept my rations. That didn't mean I wanted to fast, just that my inner conflict suddenly made it too painful to continue to eat. After I had missed one, two, and then three meals, I became totally preoccupied with my empty stomach and food. I started to be really thankful for food. Gratitude tore down the walls of my inner conflict, and it sprouted a new shoot. A new skin formed over my wounds. I had an opportunity to look into the state of my soul.

Being so hungry, I had an opportunity to see the shame of my hard-shelled spiritual life. I realized that I had no right to eat a meal every day, a meal that wasn't really mine anyway. I was surprised at the simplicity, that all my thoughts were preoccupied with a craving for food. I asked myself if I had ever realized that my heart was as poor as my present stomach, longing only for God. No, I had not. I had measured the world with my own eyes, by my own ruler, and was in despair. To despair is an act of arrogance toward God, overriding God's authority and blocking prayer. Despair had filled me up, leaving no room for God to speak to me. I had learned that faith means to trust God rather than oneself, but I had not pursued that. I had not let God be God. My judgment and despair blocked my thinking process. I had judged the world from my own perspective. My unplanned fasting developed into the fasting of repentance, and repentance crumbled the walls of despair.

I asked myself probing questions. Do you think that what you see and hear and know is everything there is? You cannot see the universe and understand the earth that contains you and moves around the sun and rotates by itself. "For my thoughts are not your thoughts, neither are your ways my ways, says the Lord. For as the heavens are higher than the earth, so are my ways higher than your ways and my thoughts than your thoughts" (Isaiah 55).

My soul was asking endless questions of why, regarding afflictions and calamities, but I began to realize that silence is the beginning of emptying my thoughts and questions and of filling God in me. The silence in itself is a prayer and a stepping-stone to enter into God's presence.

I began to see my arrogance in being indignant about my powerlessness and my inability to solve the miseries of the human condition around me. I forgot the truth that life is not based on its own condition, but on God's covenant with his people. Repentance broke open a dike of held-back tears and reinforced a prayer in which I was ready to offer my precarious life back to God.

The days have become shorter, and darkness comes quickly. I eventually got permission from the hospital authority to go in after work to visit the tents to witness and to hold worship services. (First, though, I pray fervently outside the tent.) Not only am I allowed my pastoral care, but I am also offered special favors to receive the supplies needed for my activities. I feel so thankful for that. Did man plan that by himself? No. God prepared everything and waited for me.

I have started to visit the surgical ward, where most of the patients know me. Except for a few officers, most of patients are young teens. Their bodies are haggard, bony, drab, and swollen; but their eyes are clear and shiny.

My dear friend, you can easily imagine their faces—the faces of our younger brothers. They were born of parents who had lived under Japanese oppression. They are boys who should have been playing and learning at school and nurturing their dreams. Among them are clever boys with straight foreheads, sparkling eyes, closed lips, and a determination to overcome hardships. Most of them are still playful and eager teenagers, just now developing their physical maturity; yet many have now lost their arms or legs. Their dreams and hopes have been ruined. Can we call them POWs? Can we brand them war criminals?

They welcomed my appearance with a smile and asked for medicine. I stood there and opened my mouth cautiously. "I have brought medicine which is not taken internally or applied externally, but which will give you peace. I won't talk. I will sing hymns and read the Bible for you. You just remain where you are on the beds and listen, please." I prayed shortly in silence and began singing.

All the way my Savior leads me.
What have I to ask beside?
Can I doubt his tender mercy,
who through life has been my guide?

Before I'd finished one verse, someone screamed like a thunderbolt: "Be quiet! Shut up!"

The voice was shockingly loud. The voice seemed not just to detest hearing the hymn or to reject me, but to be a desperate wailing. It was not the voice of rage but a death throe. When I saw the source of the scream, I was shocked again. He was a handsome officer with his right arm amputated. I remembered that his last name was Chung. He used to be quiet, expressionless. But now, his whole body spouted a fountain of melancholy and anxiety, too transparent and unapproachable for us.

The reason I remembered his last name is that he spoke fluent English. One day when the US surgeons were making their rounds, the officer blurted out, "Because you don't show compassion, we cannot trust you." He did not express any enmity toward them, nor did he expect anything from them. The doctors looked at each other in embarrassment. They were surprised at his fluent English as well as his remarks. Then he added, "You are doing us a favor. But what hurts is your attitude of superiority toward us. That does not serve any benefit or therapeutic purpose." And then he sealed his mouth. Since then, I had never seen him speak to them.

When he screamed out at me, time seemed to stop, and the silence lingered as if sucked into a vacuum. I met his gaze, and I felt my inner pillar, which barely supported me, collapse. I had nothing solid to hold on to. I slumped to the ground.

Then I heard a whispering voice: "You yourself are a source of power. A world is out there, waiting for you. You can make money, enjoy married life, attain honor, and have children. You were born to enjoy life."

But a young soldier shook me and whispered, "Sir, please stand up. The officer is lonely. He cries out because he is lonely. Let's sing together and give praise, for God is weeping with us." And he started to sing, his face wet with tears. He had just one leg, bushy hair growing out of a shaven head, a clean and charming face. The officer who had screamed turned his back on us, but I could see his trembling.

Then the answer came from God: "I am who I am." God, who is too big for us to see, nonetheless cares for each small thing, even though we cannot see him with our human eyes. I rose and made new steps toward God.

After that incident, I continued my visitations to the wards, but there was always strong jeering. "Hey, hey, you said, 'Jesus and heaven.' It's ********! Stop it. I don't want to hear it anymore."

The weather became cold, and I noticed that some prisoners were hopping around in bare feet, trying not to touch the cold ground. The Americans had provided plenty of shoes, and they had diligently and abundantly delivered such supplies. But here they were, walking barefoot, and I wondered what they had done with their shoes and socks.

Then one day I found out that people from the outside were bringing such commodities as sushi, taffy, liquor in small glass bottles, rice cakes, and cooked sweet potatoes to the barbed-wire fence. People inside the camp approached the barbed wire with socks, shoes, and occasionally unstamped underwear to exchange for the savory food items they craved.

How strange to see a person exchange a pair of shoes for a loaf of sushi or a rice cake. Bargaining and shouting took place across the barbed wires, and I found myself among the crowd of people, standing on tiptoe, shoving and being shoved, and reaching out our hands, achieving only a moment of satisfaction while the people outside earned some petty cash.

I tried to make sense of why I was here. I knew I should not venture out until I saw, knew, and comprehended more. There was only one way to prevent them from gobbling up shoes and underwear, and I looked up to heaven and prayed, "For he will hide me in his shelter in the day of trouble . . . to behold the beauty of the Lord, and to inquire in his temple" (Psalm 27).

Sincerely,
Mang Eui-Soon

The Wilderness Church

NOVEMBER 1950, A FROSTY DAY

I have some important news. I met Lee Hoe-Jin here. He used to attend our Bible class for middle-school students. You might recall him—slender, charming, with an excellent voice. He was dressed in a baggy POW uniform when he came to see me at the hospital headquarters.

"Mr. Mang." He hugged me. I felt his upper body trembling and thought he was crying. But then I realized he was laughing.

"Now it's all right. I knew that I would find you here. God led us here as a shepherd drives his sheep into a sheepfold." He was confident, and his tearful eyes were laughing. He still had the clean face of a young teen, but he looked more matured than in his church school days.

He told me his story. On graduation from high school, he worked for the American International Telephone Company. When the Korean War broke out, he thought that the "old man," Korean president Rhee, would need him when he wanted to make phone calls to the United States, so he bravely stayed on the job. When he heard someone was needed to repair the phone system in the Taejon telephone office after it was bombed, he volunteered to go there. En route to Taejon, he was captured by Communist volunteers. He surrendered to UN forces around the Honam province and was sent here immediately. When he arrived here, this was a camp in name only; it was still a barren desert lacking accommodations and facilities. Since then, so many improvements were made that it seemed like paradise.

Now, he was comparatively happy living the prisoner's life. In addition, thanks to his ability to speak English, he was assigned to the prisoner review committee to keep files and records.

Lee Hoe-Jin laughed and confidently confided in me, "Although I was captured and am imprisoned in this place, I believe there is a definite will and meaning for this. Just recently, I met Park Yong-Ki working at the meal tent in the fifth camp, and he told me about you. I thought, *Aha! God has a great sense of humor.* Mr. Mang, now that I see you here, I have a strong feeling that something important is happening."

I felt the living presence of the Lord in so many encounters. Joy energized my body. One after another, friendly faces began to appear, like stars in the night sky. I found a senior student of Choson Seminary working at POW company headquarters, and I heard through the grapevine that there were many other people here. God again gave me a reason to smile through the presence of Lee Hoe-Jin.

Sincerely,
Mang Eui-Soon

November 1950, on a moonlit night

A church has been built here on barren land. A cross has been raised over the tent beside the ward that accommodates the patients. We called her the Wilderness Church to remind us that we are in the wilderness. Park Yong- Ki, Lee Hoe-Jin, Pastor Koo (a senior student at Choson Seminary), and I obtained pieces of wood to make a pulpit and chairs.

At our first worship service we praised God with tears of joy. We also envisaged the wilderness lying ahead of our people before we can reach Canaan, the Promised Land. I pray that this church will be the tabernacle of our people in the wilderness.

While building this church, we suffered much scorn and ridicule. "Stop this complete nonsense! Be what you are: prisoners. Have they said they'll let you out if you hold on to the Yankee's Devil? It would be better to offer a sacrifice to the spirits,[1] so we can have rice cakes."

As they ridiculed us, I thought about Noah. While Noah was building the ark, people were enjoying banquets and parties and weddings and building up their wealth. They scorned him and wagged their fingers at him as if he were crazy! Then Noah went into his ark one sunny day, and seven days later the flood covered the earth. What do these seven days mean? God waited seven days for the people on the earth, who were full of wickedness, to return to him. He allowed them a last chance before destroying the earth.

Maybe this prison camp is like those seven days after Noah entered the ark. This could be the last chance given to us. We don't consider ourselves to be as righteous as Noah. We believe that the door is open to anyone who wants to enter into the ark of grace. It's our responsibility to shout

---

1. In Korean culture, food and alcoholic beverages are traditionally offered to the spirits of dead ancestors. This is a ritual expression of respect, and after a formal presentation, these items are then shared by the participants in a celebratory feast.

at them at the top of our lungs that the ark of grace waits for them.

Yours sincerely,
Mang Eui-Soon

Enter the Communist Chinese

January 1951

One cold, windy day toward the end of the year, packed truckloads of refugees were unloaded along the other side of the barbed wire like troops of ants pushed from an excavated anthill. Most of them wore layers of clothing, and some carried parcels on their backs or heads. We could tell that they had left their homes in a rush.

"Where are you all coming from?" someone asked.

A middle-aged woman holding on to the barbed wire responded in a heavy Hamkyung province dialect, "I boarded a boat in Heongnam. Where are we now?" After a brief exchange of information, she anxiously asked, "Ah, do you know Kim Chang-Ma, a young guy?" Her words were a catalyst for an outpouring of heartbreaking inquiries from all quarters. People on both sides crowded around, screaming and craning their necks to look for people they knew. When those on our side learned that these people were countrymen of Hamkyung province, there was a boisterous commotion of people speaking the Hamkyung dialect.

They had put on as many layers of clothing as they could, including hats of dog or rabbit hair. Their faces were greasy and dirty, as if they hadn't had showers for a long time. Their eyes were shining with the joy and relief of being alive, although they were cold and hungry and afraid. Strangely enough, some wore a familiar US Army steel helmet on top of their winter hat. It made us laugh to see the helmets wobbling on their heads.

Amid the shouts, someone inside the barbed-wire fence was curious about the helmets. "Where did you get the helmets? Did the US soldiers give them to you?" he called again and again.

Finally, someone answered him: "They were strewn all over the road. This is a very useful thing. I can use it as a bowl as well as a chamber pot. If I survive, I will keep it as a household treasure."

The helmets must have been taken from dead American soldiers. It is unthinkable for live soldiers to give up their helmets, so they were probably taken from dead soldiers as they lay in a field, by the roadside, or in the mountainside, neither knowing nor caring that someone was taking off their helmets.

Imagine! These refugees, taking a perilous route by boat, carried the helmets, initially worn by US soldiers, and now were using them as bowls as well as chamber pots. And someday they would set them aside as household treasures with no thoughts for the soldiers who wore the helmets.

"We can't afford to be concerned about the dead. It's nonsense," some might say if you asked about that. "Let's not bother with anything serious while we are still alive." This is what their faces told me. It was frightening to see humans that cold hearted. Who and what made them like that?

A bone-chilling wind came from the north. The news that Seoul had fallen into the hands of the enemy made us even colder. If our troops had not been defeated so fast, I might have had a chance to hear about my parents and you and other friends. And I know my parents and you will be anxious to hear about me. I shudder to think that poor Seoul is again in the hands of the enemy and undergoing further hardships.

The Chinese Communists had attacked like a tidal wave. They rushed into a land already burned several times by the fires of war. Their intervention slashed any optimistic views on the war. At a conservative estimate more than 1.2 million Chinese soldiers poured into Korea. Their airpower, communication equipment, artillery, and transport equipment were very poor, so they walked, mostly at night. Armed with assorted rifles made in Russia, Japan, or the United States, they crossed over the rough mountains, carrying food and ammunition on their backs. Their communication system was made up of bugles, flutes, and drums. Our troops were baffled at not being able to spot them.

Oxen or horses carried military supplies, but when these were unavailable, they carried rifles, mortars, and machine guns on their own heads. But still they moved as if they were running. They couldn't carry middle-range cannons, so these were left behind. At dawn, they concealed everything. At dusk, they started to move in a huge, devilish mass. They crossed the Yalu River so craftily that the

American air force, which flew over North Korea every day, did not notice.

Sometimes I become impatient. I enjoy more freedom than any others inside the camp; I have better food and receive clothes and personal care supplies earlier than others. But I ask myself if I am giving my all to them in return for these privileges. I stopped eating in the hospital and started dining with the prisoners at the general food service. The time after work and before sleep is so short to visit the patients' tents, and I must also think of the others. Lee Hoe-Jin is working full-time as a caretaker of the church. The three of us, including Kang Hui-Dong, visit the tents for prayers, and it has become our evening routine to return to the church for prayers after the night roll calls. "Stay awake and pray. Stay awake and pray," I am ceaselessly hearing the Lord say.

A few nights ago, two patients passed away. No one stayed with them. They all hate the dying for inviting the god of death to them, so instead of extending condolences or praying for their souls, they brand them an omen of misfortune and send them hatred or frowns to fend off the bad luck. The exuberant and genuine joy of family and friends at their birth ends here with a burial in strange frozen soil and a few scoops of dry earth.

Since that night I usually go around the patient tents at one or two in the morning and check on them. Some paramedics are around, but they seldom help the patients in trouble; they fulfill only their assigned job. We have civilian doctors and nurses coming from outside to help us, but they have very tight schedules in the surgery room and hospital headquarters. There just isn't enough staff to fully care for patients through the night.

I walk through the different areas, carrying gauze, cotton balls, and antiseptics supplied by the hospital. The paramedics snore under a dim, incandescent light and don't bother me. Patients who have passed a critical stage manage to sleep in peace in the cold, dark night, but the serious ones are a different case; they continue to grapple with their pains in the face of a menacingly imminent death.

"Lord, you are watching these people. Have mercy on them and strengthen them with your power of love and life. Have them see you through their sufferings. Touch your hands on them so that they are able to sleep."

I pray ceaselessly as I exchange the pads or clean the bloody pus or massage the painful parts of the body. It's not me; I just make myself available to the Holy Spirit, who is working in me. When I finish with one patient, I move over to another one, wiping my hands thoroughly with antiseptics. Sometimes when I clean their faces and hands with hot water and pray for them aloud, I see tears flowing down their cheeks. I cry when I see them fall asleep peacefully. I affirm with thankfulness the love and power of the Lord. I know that his presence is with us through all this misery. He washes our affliction with his tears. I am so joyful for the grace that gives me understanding.

Sometimes I look at the starry sky on a cold winter night. Wiping away my tears and listening, I am able to hear a profound mystery of heaven. Oh, my friend, there is nothing in this world that God has made that is not beautiful. I am amazed at the mystery of starlight, traveling for several light-years to reach my eyes. In praising the Lord, I overcome misery. My dear friend, I see you in the starlight. I am enabled to believe that wherever you are, I am with you, and it reassures me to think that your spirit is beside me. Don't be sad, and keep active.

Sincerely,
Mang Eui-Soon

The Visit of Captain Yu

February 1951

Dear Friend,

Today for the first time I visited a camp of Chinese Communist POWs. Every day they are unloaded, and among them are many invalids. These Chinese are mostly simple, naive country kids and have only the clothes they came in. They looked different from us, with prominent cheekbones and wondering eyes taking in their surroundings. They exhibited neither fear nor hostility, staring at me without any emotion, as if they were seeing strangers with a strange culture in a strange land.

Who could call them Communists? Carrying antiquated rifles, these country kids had walked thousands of miles to the front on a loaf of rice or a piece of wheat cake without even knowing why they had been conscripted. They walked, hid, and battled like work oxen without complaining or questioning why their government called them to war. They moved as they were told to move and seemed unaware of any difference between east and west. Even though they had been taken as POWs, they were still being fed and cared for, and their biggest worry now seemed to be about whether these new people might be mad at them.

Many suffered frostbite, and their feet or hands had to be amputated, even though they had no gunshot wounds. Their quilted uniforms seemed very old and worn out and white with the enormous amount of DDT powder for personal hygiene. As the patients received their supplies, including new uniforms, and were transferred to other tents, they jumped for joy like children and giggled when they saw their old clothes being burned in the fire. They were relaxed because they were fed, kept warm, and did not have to use rifles or walk. They didn't seem like strangers but like neighbors from a long time ago.

Because of the language barrier, they presented problems for the medical personnel. I wanted to speak to them, and they wanted to say something to me. I chose as an interpreter a Chinese POW who claimed to speak English, but communication with him was very difficult.

I had two strange feelings when I first met the Chinese POWs. They are not enemies invading our country with rifles, but sheep that God has driven along. By that I mean that God has called them here. I envisioned myself kneeling to serve them. I tried to ignore the idea, to treat it as nothing, but the vision compelled me to kneel. I asked its interpretation. I wanted to shake myself out of that vision, but I couldn't. Someone was holding me down firmly.

That night, when I visited them, I began to realize a very important and serious truth. God had started the work of salvation on billions of Chinese people living behind the iron curtain. The iron curtain was a man-made evil, but God had led these young men out from their captivity. We had to sow the seed of the gospel in their hearts. How wonderful is God's plan! Through the wonderful grace of God I have been entrusted with this opportunity.

Think about the Western missionaries who went into the jungles of Africa or South America, risking their lives and encountering so many hardships. We know that many missionaries suffered persecutions bringing the gospel to us. Comparing the pains they suffered, how easy it is to bring the gospel to these Chinese people who are now so close to us. Oh, how wonderful it is! Our suffering caused by the Korean War has opened up a morning of blessings. I believe that, and I give thanks to God.

Sincerely,
Mang Eui-Soon

MARCH 1951

My Dear Friend,

A new alley has been made outside the barbed wire surrounding the women's prison camp, segregated from the men's. Not long ago women POWs were accommodated in the camp that was built on the inclined hill beside the fourth prison camp. Male prisoners would crane their necks, yelling at the women's camp to get any kind of response from them. The camp was intended to imprison the members of the women's NKPA, but quite a large number of civilian women taken during the war were added, and among them were nurses and even doctors. They tried to help each other, but because of differences in ideology, in previous living environments, and in emotional expression, they lived in tension.

Every Sunday, Lee Hoe-Jin and I go to the women's camp, under the watch of military police, and lead a worship service. After preaching the Word and praising God with the choir, composed of a soprano and alto from the women's camp and a tenor and bass from our camp, we come back to our tents.

We heard that there is another camp near us, and a church has been erected there. I believe that it is due to the hard work of Reverend Harold Vockel. His Korean name is Ok Ho-Yeol, and he and his wife are giving their lives to feed the sheep enclosed inside the barbed wire. We call him the "father of Korean POWs." He and Mrs. Vockel even planned to look after people once they were discharged from the camp.

Whenever I pray, I am amazed over and over again at the wonderful love of God that led me to this place. I am thankful to God and surprised that we could erect the Wilderness Church. God has given us a sanctuary in which to worship, sent us many Christian brothers, and revealed his will for us to plow the field and plant the gospel inside this barbed wire enclosure. I feel as if I will burst in joy, because of the fullness of gratitude and the wonder of this miracle.

"We are afflicted in every way, but not crushed; perplexed, but not driven to despair; persecuted, but not forsaken; struck down, but not destroyed; always carrying in the body the death of Jesus, so that the life of Jesus may also be manifested in our bodies" (2 Corinthians 4).

Here in the prison, those of us imprisoned through misunderstanding are waiting and waiting, because our outside contacts are strictly controlled and we are not allowed to release details of our location. Confusion reigns! Is there any other case in the history of war when civilians were captured as POWs by their own army, without justification? We can thank God from the religious perspective, but is there anything more stupid than this case?

I wished I could have news about anyone, especially my dad. Was he safe until the Seoul recapitulation? And what about my stepmom? I am haunted by thoughts of my beloved people, but there doesn't seem to be any help for me at this time. Longing is like being a naughty child who keeps on demanding. I am frustrated. You are one of those beloved.

One time, I was called to the intelligence office, and on my way there, I thought it must be some kind of formal business. But when I entered the office, Miss Yu Chung-In appeared before me, wearing an army uniform showing the rank of a Korean army captain! Her big, clear eyes were shining, but her lips and cheeks were trembling. I was so happy to see her, someone I knew.

"You are alive! Thank you, Lord, thank you," she said, her body shaking.

We exchanged greetings, but she was too moved to carry on a conversation. "What happened? Who could judge Mr. Mang a POW?"

"No, Miss Yu, I am not working as a POW but as a prisoner of God. I am working with pleasure for him."

"But this is nonsense. No, this is stupid. How can we label our people as . . ."

"Miss Yu, I have no inconveniences in my daily activities, and I give what I can with thankfulness. I believe that God sends his people where they should be. I have only one wish, that you become a prayerful, supportive friend."

Later, I heard that she had had a lot of trouble getting permission to visit me. However, she actually had a mission that was much harder than the visitation itself. She had to inform me that my father had been taken to North Korea. Unable to bring herself to tell me in person, she left a note in the intelligence office before leaving. In it she explained that after I left Seoul, my father bravely followed a policeman from the North Korean Interior Affairs Office to confront him. That was the last time he was seen. About 250,000 people were slaughtered or taken to the North or lost after the Communists invaded the South. They were branded reactionaries, and my dad was likely one of them.

She had visited my stepmom with some food and had asked her to join in fleeing, but she adamantly insisted on remaining, saying, "How can I leave home now? Someday Elder Mang and Eui-Soon could come home." Miss Yu went on to say that she didn't know how my stepmother could have endured the hardships of last winter when the Chinese Communists rushed in and food was scarce.

She concluded by saying that she is working at the Third Army Hospital in Busan and that she feels her most urgent mission is to tell my stepmom about me. She will do so if she finds someone who is going to Seoul.

March 1951

Dear Friend,

The ice is melting away, and I cannot hear kids giggling as they play on the ice anymore. Is spring coming? We've had an unusually cold winter, which made it more difficult for the wounded. The refugees with neither food nor extra clothing nor a place to sleep are frozen to their bones.

The place where I kneel in prayer is still frozen, and sometimes I pound the frozen ground with my fists until they bleed. The miserable reality I face each day I experience as agony and affliction, and I must fight ceaselessly for my sanity. I believe that Jesus prays for you and me, holding us in his wounded hands. My soul is comforted when I realize that somewhere you too are praying unceasingly for me. Sometimes I dream I am a bird, an unknown bird, released from out of the barbed wire to look for you.

Sincerely,
Mang Eui-Soon

March 1951

Dear Friend,

I have no idea when you will get my letter, but I have to tell you about some important issues. On March 16, I heard that we had recaptured Seoul. How many lives have been lost to the cold? How many things have we lost that are needed for our survival? And how many gruesome fights have we been engaged in without knowing why?

Recently, I heard about some strange things from the Americans, things I was able to confirm from newspapers brought to me by a volunteer civilian doctor. How did the Registration of National Defense Force end up in such absurdity? They called up 500,000 men from the ages of seventeen to forty and trained them as a defense force, but they retreated just a few days after its formation. They retreated, not as an organized team, but as a huge mass of beggars. Most of them starved or froze to death. They were young or middle-aged men, forced to leave their parents, wives, and children. But with no supplies, neither food nor clothing, they had to beg for food, and half of them were in serious trouble with frostbite.

Our government should subsidize them. The American government still gives war expense aid to our government, and government funding for the army has been more or less dispensed, supposedly for food, clothing, medicine, and other supplies needed for the soldiers. So where have the supplies and money gone?

The executive officers embezzled the money with impunity, while the soldiers were forced to retreat, with no food for three or four days at a time in the cold winter weather. Considering such corruption, misappropriation, and embezzlement by executives of the Defense Forces, I have to wonder who the real enemies are! It's also been confirmed that a few members of parliament have received bribes from these accused executives. I am just dumbfounded. What does this mean for the future of our country? I wonder if you could find ten righteous people in positions of trust in the whole country. Because of this, our country is probably on the brink of destruction.

The course this country is taking may be calling for discipline or suffering. "Have you not brought this upon yourself by forsaking the LORD your God, when he led you in the way?" (Jeremiah 2). As these words indicate, I believe that we have brought discipline and suffering upon ourselves by our wickedness and apostasy. "Your ways and your doings have brought this upon you. This is your doom, and it is bitter; it has reached your very heart" (Jeremiah 4).

They had hearts of stone, incapable of change. Still, have they no sense of their wickedness and apostasy and no perception of their evil? Oh Lord, help me to find a righteous person, then another, until I find ten to save this country. Have mercy on our people; please, have mercy on us.

My friend, please pray for me. Help me with your prayers so that I don't feel so alone and powerless. Pray for me so I strive to become a man of prayer to confront bravely every evil I meet on this earth.

Sincerely,
Mang Eui-Soon

Freedom Refused

Chang Hyung-Jin picks up the story here:

I met Captain Yu Chung-In on April 11, the day after the US government dismissed General Douglas A. MacArthur. This had put the whole city of Busan in an uproar. We thought that the United States felt stuck in the war, unable to swallow or spit. Twenty days ago, our troops recaptured Seoul, but the fierce Chinese attack made it impossible to predict tomorrow.

I met Captain Yu, who was dressed in a neat army uniform, at a quiet coffee shop by the Yeongdo Island seashore. Facing each other we could not speak, even a simple greeting seemed too banal, and we could not find the right words to describe our feelings. Finally, I asked, “Did you see Mang Eui-Soon?”

“Yes.”

That was not just an answer. It was the release of long-held emotion. Tears poured down her face; I couldn’t say anything. Looking out at the sea, I suddenly started sobbing myself, finally letting go my own suppressed tears, lost in my own thoughts.

Our sadness was not only for the misery of the war being fought, but for brother killing brother and the lack of trust between our government and our people. The war had settled into a stalemate following the embezzlement by executives of the National Defense Force that had caused our soldiers to starve and freeze on the roads. Dramas involving the corruption and incompetence of government officials and the dirty game of politics took place daily. We young people have no leader. To whom can we go with our grievances? Who cares about our tears? We reaffirm each other and cry together.

“How is he doing?” I asked.

“He looks all right, but I don’t know. It is strange that he looked so comfortable in such a desolate place, as if it were his home. He wore a uniform with ‘POW’ stamped on it in white paint, and yet he looked so peaceful, but tired.”

"When do you think visitation will be permitted for family or civilian guests? And what about correspondence?"

"Actually, the Security Department reviews letters, but I know someone who works at the department, so my private letters are permitted to a certain degree. My army uniform helps. Nonetheless, in order to make one visitation, I wasted several trips. It is extremely difficult."

"It would be almost impossible for me to see him?"

"Well, if the war ends dramatically . . ."

I was surprised at this comment and said, "There will be big trouble if the war should end like that. There are quite a number of people whom the Americans indiscriminately threw into prison. Whether they had fled because they were anti-Communists, refugees, students, or farmers, they didn't even try to find out. If the war ends without a safe way to sort out these prisoners, Mang Eui-Soon might be forcibly taken back to North Korea."

Listening, her eyes flashed. "From now on, we should make every effort to get Mr. Mang released. I will contact the Security Department. I want you to check with the church, school, and the US Eighth Army Intelligence Office. We will do whatever we can."

The hope planted in our hearts was a little lighthouse shining in the dark, a star in the sky. We felt commissioned to strive for his release. This young man had deserted the North to flee to the South. He and his family were Christians who had fled to escape the Communists. He had been a seminary student, a teacher of the middle-school class in Namdaemun Church, and a pastor in charge of the church in the Bupyung Army Hospital, a civilian refugee who had left enemy-occupied

Seoul to seek a safe place where our troops were stationed. If we could prove all this, he would be released.

On February 1, 1951, the United Nations adopted a resolution to end the Korean War peacefully. However, North Korea continued to attack by throwing more Chinese Communist soldiers into the war. Would the war really end?

I quit trying to see Mang Eui-Soon, deciding instead to put my energy into his release. I first went to Reverend Bae Myung-Joon. He cried as he held my hands and prayed for Mang Eui-Soon. "I pray for him constantly. It was I who told him to flee south . . . I cannot help feeling guilty whenever I think of him."

Reverend Bae Myung-Joon helped us try every possible means to prove the identity of Mang Eui-Soon. More than a hundred refugee church members signed a petition asking for his release. The seminary issued copies of his student card and student registry. Captain Yu Chung-In obtained certification that Mang Eui-Soon was a chaplain at the Bupyung Army Hospital, and she met with an American minister in charge of the Christian mission at the prison camps. We were filled with hope in anticipation of his release. It was difficult to contact the intelligence office of the US Eighth Army, but after Captain Yu Chung-In exhausted all other possible means, she made it through to a friend working at the Ministry of Defense. Despite her army officer status, it took several trips in order to have one visit.

She went everywhere to find books that Mang Eui-Soon wanted, searching for special drawing paper for him to copy hymns to be used in the camp.

"I feel ashamed because I let you do all the tough jobs," I said to her.

She smiled. "No, Mr. Mang is the one who gives me the confidence to survive in this treacherous world. He is my window of hope through which I am inspired to believe that life is worth living and has meaning and value."

I agreed with her, and through her lens I saw myself. I needed him desperately. My eagerness to see him as soon as possible was the driving force behind my hard work. When they announced the armistice at Kaesong, I was to be allowed to visit him. The day we left was very hot. I waited for Captain Yu to finish her work, and then we waited impatiently at the gate for several long hours, and longer still at the security office, even after having received our security check. When we were almost exhausted, Mang Eui-Soon finally appeared to us.

He beamed, smiling as if it had only been yesterday when we last saw each other. But my heart was ready to burst. Oh my friend! There were no words. "How are you doing?" I finally asked blandly, holding and shaking his hands.

"I am fine. Even if I were to get sick, there are many doctors, nurses, and medicines around."

He changed the topic and asked questions concerning the situation of our country. I talked quickly in a soft voice, watching the guard beside us. "You don't have many days left inside. The time will come shortly when the barbed wire will be gone."

He understood immediately what I was alluding to and looked at Captain Yu and me alternately, his face beaming with a bright smile and his eyes opening wide. "Could it be real? Could that really happen?"

Before we left, we promised that we would contact his stepmother, and we shared other news about books that he wanted to read and about friends both inside and outside.

The intelligence office of US Army told us his release was feasible with just a few supplementary documents. We discussed his accommodations after his release and checked into his return to school and searched for ways to get him a certificate from the US Army permitting him to cross the river so that he could see his stepmother in Seoul and stay with her. We spent every day of July in a festive mood as we prepared for meeting him.

Then one day, when the review process by the intelligence office was almost completed and we had been informed of his imminent release, Captain Yu visited me in a panic, "I saw him today to assure him he was about to be released. He told me in a firm but quiet voice that he had met several times with staff from the intelligence office of the US Eighth Army and had already made the decision to stay in the prison!"

She was shocked and didn't know what to do. Reverend Bae was also disappointed but said, "Mr. Mang will change his mind when all the documents are complete and he is ordered to leave. Let's wait awhile."

Finally the preliminary review was complete; the intelligence office requested his signature and his release. If he submitted those documents, his release would be final. We all went to the POW camp together, but I waited at the coffee shop nearby because I did not have permission to visit him. I was shocked to see them coming back from the camp so soon. "Is something wrong?" I asked.

"We met him, but . . ." Reverend Bae replied sadly, "he wants to stay. He says he cannot leave there."

The three of us, who had exhausted all of our means for his release, felt a sort of betrayal. "Nonsense," I said, angrily.

"Everyone has been working for him, setting aside other things. Reverend Bae, didn't you tell him that?"

"I was angry at him, too. I told him that his friend Captain Yu and I had drained all our resources during the last few months to gain his release. He dropped his head and apologized, but he persisted, saying that he couldn't accept it. He said that he could not tell us the reason, but don't we know the reason? He could not leave the members of the prison camp church and the patients and the other suffering people."

Captain Yu, silent for so long, opened her mouth. "It was not what he wanted. We started the work without asking him. We did as we thought and wished. It was I who caused you and Reverend Bae so much trouble. Please forgive me. I really did not understand Mr. Mang at all. To tell the truth, I feel so silly . . ." Before she finished speaking, she began walking down toward the tramcar station.

We began to hear various rumors from inside the prison camp, concerning some gruesome incidents. The war was apparently not confined to the front. About eighty thousand Chinese Communists and North Korean POWs had been transferred since January 1 to Koje Island, and these prisoners were designated by an emergency measure for complete isolation. They had surrendered en masse, so there was a flood of people in the prisoners' camp. Chaos resulted because security guards couldn't even count such large numbers, let alone manage them. Dead bodies were often found in the washrooms. Prisoners were being beaten to death and thrown out with the sewage, blocking it up. At roll call, missing ones were recorded as runaways. A rumor spread that the Communists had formed a political structure inside the camp. Apparently, more than 50,000 North Korean POWs out of 130,000 did not want to go back home, and 15,000 Chinese POWs out of 20,000 felt the same. They said, "We'd rather die here than return to the Communist regime."

More than half of the North Korean POWs had surrendered intentionally and were commissioned for particular tasks. One of their objectives had been to reduce the number of our troops at the front by creating the need for more troops to guard the increased number of prisoners. Some of these infiltrators plotted riots and other disturbances inside the camp. They intended to search out the POWs who did not want to return and control them by force and create an advantageous position whenever armistice talks started, by making all sorts of accusations. This well-planned manipulation by the infiltrators worked to make the camp "Red," spread false rumors, and foment unrest among the prisoners. Two of the rumors were: "The US forces are experimenting with poison gas, biological weapons, and atomic bombs on the POWs," and "They are taking POWs to Japan, or Tsushima, or islands in the Pacific Ocean for forced labor or for use in experiments with chemical weapons."[2]

Representatives of the International Red Cross and the Neutral Nations Supervising Commission (NNSC) woke up to this Communist propaganda. They conducted regular inspections of the camp in Koje Island with suspicious eyes and were

---

2. Joseph C. Goulden, *Korea: The Untold Story of the War* (New York: Times Books, 1982), pp. 599–604.

extremely sensitive to the issues of the human rights and interests of POWs. They were angry that they could not inspect the POW camp in North Korea. Members of the press from free countries had access to the camp and sent articles and photos of the activities of POWs inside the camp to the whole world. The Communist camps were shrewd and manipulative and Western camps gullible and naive. The Communists' agreement to an armistice resulted from their newly adopted tactics, and they did not intend to end the war. They planned a conspiracy behind the curtain of armistice, which many people did not comprehend.[3]

It was at this time that I received a letter from Mang Eui-Soon.

Insurgence within the Prison Camp

APRIL 1951

Dear Friend,

Please forgive me. I am writing this letter as I kneel in prayer and fold my hands. I am entreating in tears for Reverend Bae and Captain Yu to accept my apology.

Under difficult circumstances, the three of you spent months of your valuable time preparing many documents and petitions required for my release. How can I make a proper apology for rejecting your favors and love? I am ashamed and sorry for all the inconveniences. Please,

3. Joseph C. Goulden, *Korea: The Untold Story of the War* (New York: Times Books, 1982), pp. 587–99; Max Hastings, *The Korean War* (London: Pan Books, Ltd., 1988), pp. 377–87.

at the very least, understand that my reason for staying came from my resolution to love the brothers and church members. I feel so peaceful here as if hiding in a fortress. I am thankful to God for allowing a wretch like me an opportunity to live with such good people. What would I do if I were out of this place? From time to time, I recollect a prayer of St. Francis of Assisi.

> Lord, as long as I am aware of the hell that exists, how could I enjoy heaven? Lord, have mercy on those who are condemned, and call them into heaven, or send me to hell to comfort those who suffer. I would descend to hell to establish orders for those who suffer. And if I could not lighten their suffering, I would stay in hell to suffer with them.

But this place is not hell. Enclosing a place with barbed wire does not create hell. Whether it is within or without the enclosure, that place becomes hell when people cease to love. This place, where they need me, may be easier for me to stand than the jostle and bustle of the outside. If I were thrown into that arena, I might not be able to cope with the problems and conflicts. Actually, I am a coward, living in limited freedom and amazed at how quickly I have become acclimatized to the simplicity of obligation this freedom brings about. The routine activity here utterly eliminates unnecessary trivialities, especially in the realm of thinking. It is monotonous, but I have progressively settled into it.

I have a couple of requests. First, please write a note to my stepmom who spends her lonely life in Seoul. Next, please tell Captain Yu, respectfully, to keep her visitation on hold. Her visits cause too much trouble for her and receive undeserved misunderstanding, insults, and embarrassment. I cannot bear her suffering, and it really breaks my heart.

I believe that you, dear friends, have so much to do for our devastated country without having to spend time and effort on my behalf, since I am really doing all right. We need only reaffirm each other with our eyes and with a touch of our hands. In spirit, I am with you and Captain Yu always, and also with my dad, who is a captive under the northern sky or is resting in heaven, along with my mother, two sisters, and an older brother, who managed to escape this disastrous war by departing just in time.

I weep in gratitude for your love and blessing. We see each other in our prayers.

Yours sincerely,
Mang Eui-Soon

OCTOBER 1951

My Dear Friend,

Yesterday, we were panic stricken inside. Someone who was suspected of being an informer was murdered in broad daylight. Some POWs beat him to death right in front of a large crowd. It is quite clear that Communist cadres have infiltrated our camps. It is hard to recognize who the members are, but the authorities are watching each prisoner's behavior carefully and recording it in detail to determine who are the enemies among us. In human history I have never known of a place where two nations exist together in a war camp, except here. How could such an outrageous thing happen in this country? Groups or parties that trample on or kill those who do not obey them are forming in the war camp. We often observe them tying messages to stones and throwing them over to the adjacent camp or using hand signs, whistles, or signal flags for their communications. The prison guards have a hard time controlling the prison and seem to want to give up on their duties. Some of them become so impatient that they want to use force against the Communists ("an eye for an eye and a tooth for a tooth"), and it is not easy to control the anger. The human conscience seems so weak, and goodness is easily crushed down by evil.

I had a chance to browse through some US magazines, which are distributed here for the American soldiers. I was surprised at the lavishness and luxury. I am sure that not all Americans enjoy such a lifestyle, but the food, clothing, and merchandise shown seemed sybaritic.

Many of the young people feel completely isolated, since we cannot rely on the Americans anymore. What is strange to us is that most of the students who attended college in Seoul openly confess their sympathy for the Communist cause. At the same time, there are POWs from the North asking their captors for protection. As I indicated in a letter I sent to Captain Yu, we need closer contact with our own army guards, and if you find someone who can get things moving, we would like him to warn the authorities of our camp situation as quickly as possible. Please consider our country's needs and help us. I believe that only the power of prayer can console my fearful brothers.

Sincerely,

Mang Eui-Soon

Although Mang Eui-Soon's letter had been written in a hurry, each character was done with excellent penmanship. Yet this letter indicated the urgency of the situation inside the camp. When I met with Captain Yu, she said she had exhausted all possible means of making the situation inside the camps known. "I challenged the authorities and implored them to do something, but most of them seemed too absorbed in other things to even listen to me."

She also continued to visit Mr. Mang, although he had asked her to stop going there. In November, as late fall turned to winter, Captain Yu fell sick. I received a letter around that time.

NOVEMBER 1951

Dear Friend,

Peace was restored to the camps. Storm clouds were removed with the sudden transfer of certain POWs, just as the extremists were on the verge of exploding, but it also meant that members of the Wilderness Church became scattered.

Our classmates from the seminary were moved to another camp, along with many choir members, so now our only members are from North Korea. I worry that those who had to leave might be allocated to a place where the Communists are active. The Communists' firm resolve is that they will eliminate those who have become associated with our armed forces or with the church. Of course they also want to destroy the church.

Copies of the hymnbooks written on special drawing paper give a new dimension to our worship services on Sunday and Wednesday nights. I have made ten handwritten copies. Now, even though the electric lights have gone, by lamplight we still sing our praises powerfully and in unity. I know that all supplies are so scarce and that you are experiencing difficulty in meeting your daily needs, and yet I keep receiving many presents. I can hardly express my thanks to you.

I heard that Miss Yu is sick. What an angel that she should be pouring out such love on me! I do not deserve it. Could you please take time to visit her in my place? I suffered from malaria last summer, and perhaps she has the same illness. There is a medicine, dispensed by the American doctor here. Remind her that the white pills are quinine; she must take three per day, one in the morning, one at noon, and one in the evening for fourteen days (this is very important). I wrote separately, but you could remind her.

Sincerely,
Mang Eui-Soon

December 1951

My Good Friend,

After snow flurries the temperature dropped below zero. The swamp has frozen, and the children are having fun on the ice, giggling and playing. I heard that the young South Korean war prisoners transferred to Koje Island had their status designation changed from POWs to civilians. I wonder what more is required for them to be free, besides just acknowledging the fact that they are no longer POWs.

I do not understand why this harbor city, located at the southern tip of a peninsula, is so freezing cold. Last winter, I didn't notice the weather so much because all my attention was on running for my life. I worry about how the refugees will find enough firewood to get through this winter. We have two oil stoves in our tents, and our church and hospital are supplied with plenty of firewood, so we are cozy. We benefit from the Americans, who enjoy rich resources and supplies, but the benefit is materialistic only. It is too much to expect spiritual or mental encouragement from them. They live under different circumstances, and their lifestyle and way of thinking are not like ours. They have no trouble carrying on their lifestyle here, but it is so different from our own, that we just watch them in amazement.

I am becoming skeptical about the outcome of what they have achieved so far. What is the foundation of the United States, the most powerful country in the world today? When their ancestors were aboard the *Mayflower* with their empty stomachs, they had only the Bible. Their hunger brought about humility, and the new land of America became their blessing. Their daily lives were devoted to prayers and praising with a pure conscience and with sincerity. But greed crept into their hearts as they stood before the vast expanse of fertile land. This greed brought about the sin of enslaving blacks and in mistreating the people who were there prior to their arrival. But still, they have some religious conscience that seems to inspire them to try to resolve international lawlessness and trouble. Though they pursue peace, can they really attain true peace? I am sure that true peace comes about only through that love they say they are cherishing, believing, and witnessing. But rather than embracing the love, they are swollen with pride in their capability of making things happen. America is no longer a country witnessing the spirit of Christianity and promoting harmony with neighboring countries. It has become a country promoting materialism and technology, teaching other countries to spend lavishly and recklessly.

I lament: this is not suffering; neither is it persecution for the Lord. I am not doing anything that could be called "dying for the Lord." Nurture me with prayer so that I can build up love and power. Prayer is the only awesome fertilizer.

Sincerely,
Mang Eui-Soon

Foiled Attempt to Murder God's People

It was January 1952 when I received the following letter. It fell into my hands a week after he had written it.

Dearest Friend,

I returned to my tent, staring at the stars in the winter sky. The groans of the patients have become integrated into the very essence of my being. My soul is bruised by the bombardment of their moaning, but the brilliant starlight breathes a mysterious power into my soul. Our people shiver listlessly in the cold and in their loneliness, barefoot in an endless pilgrimage of suffering. I am curious as to what the new year will bring about for them and for me.

For some reason, I don't have my CI (civilian identification) number yet. It is issued only to South Koreans, and they say that upon obtaining a CI number, I will be transferred to Koje Island. If this doesn't happen, I will go along with the young North Korean men (including many of our Wilderness Church members) when they are repatriated in an exchange of POWs. It would be good for me to follow them, for if they are repatriated and then sacrificed in order to keep their faith, how could I remain here? It would be a blessing for me to share with them in their suffering and death. If I am permitted the honor of martyrdom, it is the way I would choose to die.

Our church membership is multiplying. As we gather to pray, we are able to feed on the green grass of God's pastures. The Bible commentary you have found for me is of great help as we feed on spiritual food. I am joyful and thankful to see you in the Lord.

Your friend,
Mang Eui-Soon

Mang Eui-Soon wrote again in February 1952.

Dear Friend,

I have obtained a CI number, but I don't know whether to be excited or not because of the hundreds of North

Korean members of our church who are dependent upon me. With my CI number I am designated to go to Koje Island, but the American doctors have circumvented this by declaring that I have dysentery and must be hospitalized here. I am thankful that I am allowed to stay here and serve the church and the brothers more fervently. Since no visits are permitted until the end of March, I might not send you letters as I usually do via Miss Yu. I also reminded Miss Yu of the change in the visitation schedule, but you could remind her so that she does not waste her time.

Sincerely,
Mang Eui-Soon

Chang Hyung-Jin takes up the narrative:

On May 7, 1952, Francis T. Dodd, a brigadier general and the commander of the POW camp in Koje Island, was kidnapped by Communist POW extremists and held hostage in the camp. The incident substantiated Mang Eui-Soon's worries. The hostage takers demanded an end to the beatings, torture, confinement, and massacres; but this was propaganda to taunt the United States. The Communist prisoners often practiced kangaroo courts and forced confessions, executing anti-Communist inmates by beating them with clubs or stoning them to death. Lynching anti-Communist dissidents was rampant in the compounds. Terror gripped the camp. After order was restored and the Communist inmates were moved to new compounds, UN troops found a staggering weapons arsenal: three thousand spears, a thousand Molotov cocktails (bottles filled with gasoline and armed with cloth wicks), forty-five hundred knives, hatchets, hammers, and metal bars. It was not just a prison camp but also an extension of the battlefield, with the enemy being provided with clothing and food and lots of time to work out strategies.[4]

After the kidnapping incident was over, Captain Yu brought me some letters from Lee Hoe-Jin and his friends who were the core members of the Wilderness Church.

> Dear Miss Yu,
>
> Greetings. May grace and peace be multiplied to you in God our Father and our Lord Jesus Christ.
>
> Since our brothers received CI numbers, or for some other reason left the church, we are at low ebb, feeling empty and lonely. But we are witnessing and that is bearing fruit, and the number of brothers has increased. We continue to live by God's grace. But the schemes of Satan are still rampant. We are living precarious lives, as if walking on ice.
>
> Don't panic, but one of our very devoted church members, Mr. Ra, conspired to kill Mang Eui-Soon and other key church members and me. He had been a high school teacher in Seoul, very intelligent and a powerful writer and speaker. We respected him and put our trust in him. He had plotted to kill all of us at the same time when we gather for early morning service, but his gang

4. Joseph C. Goulden, *Korea: The Untold Story of the War* (New York: Times Books, 1982), p. 596; Max Hastings, *The Korean War* (London: Pan Books, Ltd., 1988), pp. 382–3.

was captured, lurking after curfew the night before, and he was arrested. When the Korean security guards arrested his group, they found steel-tipped poles, knives, iron pipes, and other deadly weapons, as well a list that included Mang Eui-Soon, and us, and five other anti-Communist young men. We were at the brink of death but were saved at the last minute, and we wept hand in hand, reassuring each other.

We were really angry with the guards, but Mang Eui-Soon maintained his quiet composure. In the midst of this protest, Mang Eui-Soon slipped away, and we finally found him praying in the church by himself. We stared in amazement when we saw him. His head was bowed to the knee on the ground in prayer, and his back was to us. His posture illustrated a perfect sermon. We found out later that his prayer was not only for thankfulness for our survival, but also for Mr. Ra, who did not repent but sided with evil.

Despite being a caretaker of this church, I am always falling asleep. I am trying to find more time to sleep whenever possible. Actually, Mang Eui-Soon disturbs my sleeping. I don't know when he sleeps. After work, he preaches in the compounds and visits the hospital wards. After midnight, he visits throughout the night with patients who have serious illnesses, sometimes returning to the church at two or three o'clock in the morning to pray. We are living within the fortress of Mang Eui-Soon's prayers. As Mr. Mang says, we live in God's sanctuary, like a brood of chicks gathering together under the wings of the hen to seek protection from the vultures.

One thing that I worry about is his health. We don't know what he does all night, as he is the only one with permission to enter the wards at that time. We have heard that he prays at the bedside of patients with serious illnesses, besides serving them. He also visits the wards of Chinese patients. We eat and sleep on schedule, and even if we were allowed to visit, we know that physically we could not stand his pace.

The American doctors want to keep him here longer, providing his fake hospitalization, for their own benefit. They probably could not carry out their routine functions without him.

When we scrutinize our own position and surrounding environment, we feel desperate and hopeless, and we cannot ensure that any day will pass safely. A year ago, the peace talks that had been hastily started seemed to result in an immediate cease-fire, but the situation remains in a stalemate. It is nonsense to brand innocent people such as Mang Eui-Soon as a Communist. He did not even touch a rifle. There seems to be no hope for our release in the near future. It makes me sad that the Americans and the Korean government have kept us captive for two years.

Miss Yu, please do not tell him about our letters. We write to inform you of recent developments and to express our concerns, because Mang Eui-Soon would never speak about himself. We give thanks and praise to God our Father, who allowed us a shepherd like Mr. Mang. We pray that God's grace will be with you, Miss Yu.

Sincerely,
Lee Hoe-Jin

May 1952

Dear Miss Yu,

We met only once, but I am one of many who meet you every day through the sincere love you provide us. My name is Lee Won-Shik. I met Mr. Mang here in this wilderness where there is neither shade nor water for the soul. When I see him, in either the compound or the church, I am restored. He smiles at me, or lends me a book to read, or observes my complexion and asks if I am all right, and he prays for me.

Several nights ago, returning to the compound from work, I went looking for him in the compound office and the church, like a child looking for his mother. It was quite late, and everyone was fast asleep; the depth of the quiet startled me. But I could not find Mr. Mang.

There was a lighted compound in the distance, which housed only serious tuberculosis patients. I walked toward the light and saw him washing the feet of a patient. As I was about to enter, I panicked. This room was for tuberculosis patients—hopeless cases. I felt the room must be teeming with tuberculosis germs.

Nevertheless, there was Mr. Mang, washing the dying patients. Someone has said that a dying TB patient throws up all the germs he has carried inside. I wanted to run away, but the next thing I knew, I was rushing to rescue him, like a soldier making a dash toward the enemy line. Turning his head at my footsteps, he said with his usual kind smile, "What has happened to you so late at night?"

"I came here to get you. You should have some sleep."

"You go first, please. I will follow you," he said.

That night, Mr. Mang did not return to his compound. He knew his patient would die shortly, so he stayed to be present at his deathbed.

Miss Yu, could you please advise him to look after himself? So many sheep need Mr. Mang. We are able to survive only if he stays healthy. He almost never sleeps. His work schedule is divided into the hospital work in the day, the church administration and care for the church members in the night, the care of serious patients in the late night, and the worship service in early morning. It is a great concern to all of us, Miss Yu. Please help us.

Sincerely yours,
Lee Won-Shik

MAY 1952

Dear Miss Yu,

My name is Kang Hui-Dong. You might not remember me, but I am the one who pleaded with you that Mr. Mang not leave this camp when the issue of his release came up. I knew that even though the CI releases were not publicly announced, Mr. Mang could get out of this place informally. The reason that I opposed his release so vehemently and recklessly was that I didn't think I would have the courage to live here without him. Mr. Mang has planted a seed of faith in me, a son of a minister who didn't yet know true faith. Physically, he took care of me when I suffered a serious illness and helped me recover my strength. He restored me, physically and spiritually, to new life. It is with great sorrow, like the heavens falling, and in a total despair that I imagine being separated from him.

After Mr. Mang revoked his release, I felt so guilty that I avoided him for several days. Now I have come to myself and am struggling to find a way to get him out of here as soon as possible. The Wilderness Church, built inside a barbed wire enclosure, grows day by day and is taking root firmly. Mr. Mang should leave here as soon as possible for the outside where so many things await him. Sometimes I worry about him because he is so pure and innocent. I wonder how he will live in the treacherous world outside. But he is fully equipped with the Holy Spirit. His determination can bring about repentance and ignite the fire of the Holy Spirit in young people whose hearts are thirsty and hurting. I am so ashamed to ask, but could you please reconsider his release?

Miss Yu, you know Mr. Mang better than anyone else. He is a man of God. He was born for God's work. We'd like to keep him here, because he helps us live like men and keep our faith, but Miss Yu, please help with his release.

Sincerely yours,
Kang Hui-Dong

Completing the Journey to Canaan

Chang Hyung-Jin continues:

Ever since April 2, 1952, when the UN forces started to examine each POW regarding repatriation, Communist cadres and extremists in the Koje Island camp caused trouble. But the review and identification process continued, and anti-Communists were isolated and housed separately, although the process was slow. Communist troublemakers were separated and transferred to Koje Island, as were infiltrators disguised as patients, who had been caught. The Kojeri camp was changed to a civilian detention camp, but the hospital maintained a steady treatment load, as the total number of detainees was almost the same, because of an influx of civilians from other camps. Now the detainees in the Kojeri camp were more civilian refugees than POWs.

The Communists taunted the United Nations at the peace talks by pretending to agree to the cease-fire. Taking advantage of the stalemate situation, however, they launched attacks. Fighting resumed in every highland at the front. Despite the name change of Kojeri to a civilian camp, the chance for the release of the internees was remote until the fighting ended.

About this time, Kim Young-Joo arrived at the temporary campus of Y University on Yeongdo Island. The makeshift campus was housed in four shabby US Army tents. Rumor had it that Kim Young-Joo had been living in Daegu, or that she was married and working because it was difficult to make a living after her father, Elder Kim, had been kidnapped and taken north.

One afternoon while the blazing sun grilled the hillside of Yeonseon-Dong Neighborhood, Kim Young-Joo appeared before me again. Her face was haggard and pale, but her eyes were big and bright and lively, though filled with tears as she implored, "Could you arrange for me to meet Mr. Mang? Please help me. I heard that you have met him."

"Visitation is very difficult, but if everything goes well, he will soon be released," I told her.

"I cannot wait for his release. I have to see him. Please help me," she said. "I will pester you every day at the school, so think about that." As she spoke, she smiled from time to time, but suddenly, she broke into tears, covering her face with her hands.

When she lifted up her head, she said, "I heard that the nurse, Captain Yu, frequently sees him."

"She is an active army officer, and she goes to help the people inside."

"I have to see him. I have to. I need energy to survive. I have to see him," Kim Young-Joo said, her face tear stained.

That seemed her only goal and hope, but her wish was not fulfilled. In early August, with the summer heat at its peak, I received unexpected good news. It was the last letter Mang Eui-Soon wrote from the camp. The letter said that he was to be released and that he could not stay there any longer, even if he wanted to.

July 1952

Dear Friend,

I am about to leave here. The barbed wire has been broken down, and a new world has opened for me. Now, even if I wanted to stay here, I am to be pushed out to walk freely on good, solid earth. Even if I struggled to stay longer, I couldn't. The completed review process and stamped release documents are pushing me out. I am so thrilled that, from now on, I will be able to see those whom I wish to see anytime I want. I am already anticipating the taste of freedom with excitement. The date of my release was announced as August 12, 1952.

But why I am so excited when I leave behind those who might be taken to North Korea? Wasn't I determined to stay with them and to keep the faith to the last moment of my life? A full two years of life in this camp has been a great gift of grace to me. From now on, I should prepare for the work still needed here after my discharge. I think there is a difference between serving prisoners as a fellow prisoner and serving prisoners as a free man.

What is most beautiful is each soul we meet in Christ. Each person I meet is a wonder and a miracle. The eyes, voice, smile, words, silence, writing, and everything are so valuable to me. The meaning of this miracle is so exciting that it is likely to burst my heart.

"We are afflicted in every way, but not crushed; perplexed, but not driven to despair; persecuted, but not forsaken; struck down, but not destroyed" (2 Corinthians 4). That passage reassures me. My soul praises the Lord. My friend, we offer to the Lord all that is yet to happen as we prepare to encounter one another again.

Sincerely yours,
Mang Eui-Soon

August 12, 1952

Yes, it was August 12! We were overcome with joy and excitement. The days had passed so slowly. News about his release brought a feverish excitement to those who loved him. Captain Yu held my hands and said, "Oh Lord, thank you, thank you," but she choked on her tears and couldn't say anything more.

My mind was racing as I wondered how best to prepare for meeting my friend tomorrow. We wanted to make some preparation to welcome him, but we couldn't think clearly. All the congregation of the Namdaemun Church, refugees, and friends from the seminary had also waited for this date.

By seven o'clock in the evening, the people who had come to prepare a welcoming service were gone, except for a few who were finishing up the work for the service tomorrow. I sat looking up at the sky, and as I watched, a feeble, flickering star seemed to be reaching deep into my heart, and I felt a sense of foreboding.

A dark, ominous shadow approached the church entrance, and I was frightened. "Excuse me," a voice said. "May I see Mr. Mang's friend?" As there were no lights outside, the voice seemed somber and threatening.

"Yes. May I help you?" I responded, rising. The shadow was deadly rigid for a moment. My hair stood on end, and my voice was almost lost. "What can I do for you?"

He sobbed, staggered, and threw himself at me. "I'm Park Yong-Ki. I was the president of the student council in Namdaemun Church. I was Mr. Mang's student." It was as if mountains had collapsed. Heaven was falling. "Mang Eui-Soon has died. He has passed from us."

I could not take this in. The sky was starkly dark, a bluish purple. The flickering star turned into a painful, stabbing light that pricked my soul. I stood sobbing, staring at the sky.

Several of us helped a weeping Park Yong-Ki, half carrying him in our arms, into the church office. Then, we heard his story.

"It happened last night, no, this morning at three o'clock. At dawn, a messenger rushed to the Wilderness Church to tell us what had happened. Yesterday, all day, he led services, and at night, he went to the Chinese POW ward. There, he slipped on some water that had spilled from the basin he always used to wash the faces and feet of the patients who were in pain and could not sleep. He collapsed and was unconscious.

"I rushed to the Chinese POW ward. His torso was still wet from the spilled water. Chinese patients were awake and in a panic. They called out his name, 'Mr. Mang, Mr. Mang!' Ambulatory patients left their beds and came to his side, crying. The American doctors hurried to him. They are usually very calm and cool, but they became quite agitated. One of them closed his eyes and prayed. They patted me on the back, saying they would do their best, and not to worry too much, but to wait in prayer. They carried him to the ambulance, which rushed to the hospital in the main compound.

"Later a messenger arrived at the church and informed us that Mang Eui-Soon had died at 10:57 in the morning. Most of the doctors in the ward had gathered to discuss his case. They had exhausted every possible diagnosis, examination, and medication and finally did brain surgery, but their efforts ended in vain. The messenger said that the American doctors were very sad, and some were in tears. We gathered in the church, falling to the ground, crying and crying.

"Then, in the afternoon someone from office headquarters called me and gave me my release certificate—a day early. I was rather confused at being thrown out in this big city of Busan, where I had no one to greet me. Then I suddenly I remembered Mr. Mang had told us that following his discharge, he would go to Posu Methodist Church to meet his friend Mr. Chang Hyung-Jin."

Lonely Pilgrimage

The next day, we prepared a casket for our friend. We carried it in a hand-driven cart along the long road to Kojeri camp. The blistering heat did not let up as we walked the same road that he had walked when he was taken captive.

But at the camp headquarters someone told us, matter-of-factly, "We did not hold the dead body long. We took it out for burial this morning. We can't afford to keep bodies for three or four days for a funeral service."

"Then where did . . .?"

"It is in the POW cemetery. Because he died inside the barbed wired enclosure, he couldn't avoid the POW status. In this camp, we cannot handle a live person in the proper way, never mind a dead one. They just wrapped the body up and took it in the truck to the cemetery. I saw the car coming back almost as soon as it left. They throw a body out as they would the garbage."

We were stunned. We could not just leave, so we returned to the regimental commander. As soon as he saw us, he burst into tears. "Please forgive us. We couldn't change the rules in this camp. During the memorial service last night, everyone who knew Mr. Mang became one in tears. Every mobile patient attended the service voluntarily. Even the Chinese POWs came in crying. I came to give a eulogy, but I could do nothing but cry along with the others. This morning when the burial truck passed by, we all gathered around and sent him off with tears instead of flowers and with wailing instead of eulogies. He was so sad for those who died here, and in the end, he followed the same road as they did. I was not a Christian, but now I feel I could change my mind in my longing for him. Please forgive me. I really apologize that we had to take him to the POW cemetery."

We had no words in reply. We had no choice but to return with the empty casket, silently exchanging tearful glances with one another under the blazing summer sky. Just outside the camp, Captain Yu Chung-In collapsed by the roadside. Greatly concerned, we stopped the cart carrying the empty casket. When she recovered, embarrassed, angry, and filled with sorrow, she said, "You go ahead. I would like to excuse myself to go to the POW cemetery. It shouldn't be a problem to find his grave because he was buried just today." No one could stop her.

We prepared for the memorial service to be held in ten days on August 22, 1952. Each of us, dressed in mourning as we worked, felt cold despite the late summer heat because we had lost something valuable, as if our souls had been stripped bare. I was in charge of the musical accompaniment and had to stop several times as tears filled my eyes and flowed down my face. Then an hour before the service started, we had a visitor to our church, a young man of less than thirty years of age.

"I came here to offer this to the departed." Looking down, he thrust out two envelopes made of Chinese drawing paper.

"May I ask your name?" I asked.

As he lifted up his eyes, he said, "I knew Mr. Mang. He was a saint. Mang Eui-Soon introduced me to Jesus, or should I say, Jesus introduced Mang Eui-Soon to me. I brought this in. It is a collection of our friends' hearts. They are also having a memorial service at the same time down there. You will see when you open up the envelopes." Then he turned resolutely and disappeared through the door.

One letter in one envelope was written in Chinese in Chinese ink on Chinese drawing paper; the one in the other envelope was a translation into Korean. These eulogies, including the compact signatures of Chinese Communist patients, arrived on the right date and time of the memorial service. The letter follows.

> Offering to the Departed Mang Eui-Soon
>
> How pitiful we are, as our master of love, Mr. Mang, has passed away. As we heard that tonight a memorial service for Mang Eui-Soon is being offered in your church, we are quickly sending this heartfelt letter from all of us.
>
> We were strangers here who were not able to communicate with each other. When he came to visit our wards with the American doctors, wearing the same POW uniform as we did, we scorned him and ignored him. His smile was always warm, and his actions were sacrificial, steady, and unassuming. But we did not pay any attention

to him. Most of us were angry—at the war and at those who sent us to it.

But even in that situation, Mr. Mang showed us the way of the cross. He came to us at one or two o'clock in the morning, sang hymns to us, and taught those who could not read how to read. He carried the wooden cross and explained its meaning. In the evening after staff and personnel withdrew, Mr. Mang approached like an angel to help the patients suffering with serious illnesses. He was a like a vessel of love and mercy, receiving all our pains and groans and soothing our cries and bitterness so that we might sleep more comfortably.

He held the Bible in one hand and a water bucket in the other. He touched and massaged every part of the body of paralyzed patients. Even though we couldn't understand his prayers, they soothed our pain and induced a comfortable sleep. In winter with warm water and in summer with cold water, he washed our faces and wiped our hands and sometimes even our feet. Even when there weren't enough towels to go around, he would thoroughly wash them so that he could use a clean towel for each patient.

Mr. Mang had a mysterious power. When he washed our feet, we felt peace and comfort in our hearts. He wiped every dirty part of the body as he sang in a soft, low voice, and we began to realize and experience that there exists a God of love. We didn't have to speak the language to understand this, and he never appeared inconvenienced by our needs.

We came to understand that a group of wealthy people had exploited us. We were told we had to fight against the United States and other European countries in order to expel them. Then we realized on the firing line that we were equipped with rusty weapons fit only for the garbage, and many of our comrades died en masse. The rest of us became captives. Our arms and legs were amputated, we lost our eyes, our bodies were maimed, we became disfigured by frostbite, and we fell under the control of our enemies. Despair, grievance, and hatred hardened our hearts, and we felt hopeless.

Mr. Mang came into our hearts at that moment. His prayers melted our hearts, once cold and hard as ice, by his songs and by the soft touch of his love. Through him we came to realize that the way of the cross is love and that Jesus is the initiator of love. We learned that Jesus had to die on the cross for our sins. We studied the Bible through a comrade who interpreted Mr. Mang's messages or copied them down for us, and we learned to sing hymns. The night was not dark for us when Mr. Mang was watching over us.

When we were taken captive, we were angry and in despair, prisoners of war in the wrong place and in a strange country. After meeting Mr. Mang and learning his teachings, we were amazed at the change in our attitudes. When China expelled the gospel and built a fence as high as the sky to keep it out, God chose a few to use for his purpose and thrust us into this country. We are convinced that we did not come here to aim at Koreans with our rifles but were sent to receive the living water of the gospel in this land.

On August 11, he came to us. We could not sleep and waited for him because we had heard that he was going to be discharged. He came a little earlier, just past midnight, bringing a water bucket, a Bible, and hand-copied translations of hymns. He handed out the copies, and at the bottom of the paper, he wrote that he would be leaving tomorrow. He knelt in prayer at every bedside and washed the faces and feet of the patients with serious illnesses. While washing the patients, he sang these words in a low voice:

> God be with you till we meet again;
> loving counsels guide, uphold you,
> and with a shepherd's care enfold you,
> when life's perils thick confound you,
> put his arms enfolding round you;
> safe in his great love
> God be with you, till we meet again.
> Till we meet, till we meet,
> till we meet at Jesus' feet;
> till we meet, till we meet,
> God be with you till we meet again.

After washing the last patient, without wiping away the tears on his face, he began to read Psalm 23 to us in stammering Chinese.

> The LORD is my shepherd, I shall not want;
>   he makes me lie down in green pastures.
> He leads me beside still waters;
>   he restores my soul.
> He leads me in paths of righteousness for his
>   name's sake.
>
> Even though I walk through the valley of the
>   shadow of death,

I fear no evil;
For thou art with me;
thy rod and thy staff,
they comfort me.

Thou preparest a table before me in the presence
of my enemies;
thou anointest my head with oil, my cup
overflows.
Surely goodness and mercy shall follow me
all the days of my life;
and I shall dwell in the house of the Lord for ever.

After reading the passage, he looked up into the heavens and repeated, "My cup overflows, my cup overflows." We looked at his face and memorized that verse: "My cup overflows, my cup overflows." His peacefulness comforted us. His smile of peace was a promise to us. He rose, holding the water bucket that he used to wash the last patient. At that moment, he looked up again, as if he were recommending us to that high place before leaving, and then fell to the ground. The American doctors rushed in, and an ambulance came to take him. After dawn broke and the daily routines began, we heard that he was dead. We wept for our irresponsibility, crying, "Our insolent behavior took his life. We have caused him to die."

We know that we are not abandoned, but that we are with Mang Eui-Soon in Jesus. We know now that wherever we go or whatever we do, we have to tend the buds to blossom, to bear fruit, and to sow their seeds.

With love and respect,
the Chinese Communist ward patients of Kojeri POW camp

On the occasion of the memorial service, friends gathered. The choir sang his favorite hymn in low voices:

Where Jesus is, 'tis heaven.
Since Christ my soul from sin set free,
This world has been a heaven to me;
And mid earth's sorrows and its woe
'Tis heaven Jesus here to know.
What matters where on earth we dwell?
In cottage or a mansion fair,
Where Jesus is, 'tis heaven there.

The song called out to his friends, who came in at that point. Captain Yu Chung-In, looking pale, Kim Young-Joo, who longed to see Mang Eui-Soon but could not, Reverend Bae Myung-Joon, the young graduates from the middle school, the student council of Namdaemun Church, and the congregation and friends from Choson Seminary.

I saw Mang Eui-Soon planted in the heart of each one. He has not departed from us. His distinctive love is present in each of us.

I found the mark that Mang Eui-Soon carried in his soul present in the hearts of those who know and love him. "My cup overflows," Mang Eui-Soon smiled beside us. He whispered to me again, "My cup overflows." I nodded my head. And my soul was assured of the same mark setting me apart as he had in his soul. "My cup overflows."